AF428159

For all the creatives who showed up weekly to write.
For Stephanie, whose mirrored passion for writing and community lifts me.
For Thomas, who never doubted my voice.

Creative Kindling

52 Writing Exercises For Busy Creatives

Written by Rose Hedberg
Edited by Stephanie Shepperd
Illustrated by Shann Whitaker

Table Of Contents

Introduction

How to Use This Workbook

Either proclaimed out loud or still unearthed, you are a writer.

You carry within you a deep love for the written word. You have a narrative inside you.
A novel, a poem, a memoir, a journal entry, or maybe a six-word short story.

You've found this book because you have a desire to write.

Ideas find you in the shower or when you're driving. There is a hunger beneath your skin, a deep calling to create, but a mountain rises before you. A litany of reasons why your craft is back burner to all the other aspects of your life despite a pull to write.

- I don't have time with my job.
- I'm drained by the end of the day.
- I wouldn't know where to start.
- No one would want to read my work.
- I've never written anything outside of school or work.

I know these excuses because they were once mine. I know because I've written alongside hundreds of individuals for the past seven years who can sense a desire to write but who waver in showing up—life keeps happening, and it becomes ever more daunting to get started.

How do you move your mountain, writing creatively from a place of passion while applying the work needed to get words on the page?

You build a writing practice.

A writing practice means creating a consistent commitment of time, place, and routine as you conduct creativity. Parallel to other professional fields, practice caters to results. Athletes spend time on the field running plays. Likewise, a chemist finds answers by conducting experiments. A guitarist grows confident by strumming the strings, while a barista steams milk again and again until they understand texture by sound.

So too, in the field of writing, you bring your voice to life through an established means of repeatedly doing the work. You commit to writing over and over again to cultivate your craft. The ambiguity of this advice, however, is both a freedom and a curse. How do you start? What should you write? For how long? When? Where?

Unlike other fields of work, the regimen to build your writing muscles is widely varied. Should you follow Stephen King's commitment to writing 10,000 words a day? Or Elizabeth Gilbert's morning two-way prayer practice? Murakami's writing and running routine? You can scour the web in search of a magic potion to become a better writer, but there is no way around doing the work. Yes, to write well is to put in time, to labor your ideas into words on the page.

But here's the secret. You have permission to enjoy what you write. You have permission to write ridiculously, wacky, outrageous works. Writing is an art, a love of stories.

The ideas outlined in this workbook came from seven years of writing alongside hundreds of individuals across the globe, building a creative writing practice full of fun and experimentation. Years of trying on and altering the writing advice from literary heroes. Seven years of nudging novice writers to allow themselves the space for extraordinary play while learning the craft. You can write about animals on blind dates. Create a captain's log of exploring an uncharted planet, write a to-do list for a dictator, or a recipe for happiness.

It's all writing.

When you allow yourself to write from such pleasure, you make mistakes, you write so fast your hand cramps from the gust of ideas flowing through your fingertips, and the feeling is palpable. Writing hundreds of short stories that exist as drafts, if only to flex your writing muscles, is still writing.

The following pages are my writing practice on loan.

Where other books on writing leave you thinking about the work, the following pages, instead require action. This workbook is creative kindling for all the days you don't know where to begin. The exercises are a format to give your anxious brain a beginning as you sit at the blank page. The illustrations and themes are all the far reaches of spectacular creativity to stir your imagination. The writing advice is a whisper of things I've unearthed about writing by doing, failing, rewriting, and showing up for myself as a writer. Advice that you are welcome to skip over or inhale deeply as motivation to keep going. This workbook is creative kindling for 52 weeks, so you spend less energy staring into space and more time writing.

A few things to know before you dive in...

A writing practice varies from writer to writer, though one thing is clear. Without a defined writing practice, it is easy to sabotage creativity with excuses or worse, let the mentality of the tortured artist swallow you before you even get started. After all, Dorthy Parker is attributed as having said, "I hate writing. I love having written."[24] While novelist Paul Gallico said, "It is only when you open your veins and bleed onto the page a little that you establish contact with your reader."[12] Even Norman Mailer said, "Every one of my books had killed me a little more."[34]

Are you excited to write now?

Let's paint a picture. Imagine you have entertained an idea. You've talked about writing, and you finally get the whim to write.

You open a fresh blank page, and you adjust your space. You fidget a bit further. You allow a few words to eat away blank space in a dance of the delete key. Time ticks away, your brain drifts to a to-do list, blankness. Without a practice, the idea of writing is suddenly reared against the open landscape of actually writing. Fear slips in. A fear of the blank page. A fear of not saying the right thing, not saying anything at all, not saying anything worthy of reading. A fear of being judged, criticized because you've never written before or that you'll never write anything good. The limited time you've set aside amounts to the insistent cursor flickering, waiting for punctuation that never lands.

Sound familiar?

Imagine instead, you have the steps to get into the flow state. You have a routine to settle your doubts, inspiration to start. You have an on-ramp before jumping into the openness of an idea. You have steps breaking up the ominous idea of writing into manageable pieces. You have a set amount of time to write consistently. You have a safe space to stretch your writing muscles. You have the nitty gritty of when, where, how, and why checked off the list, so you're left with the infinite space of your imagination.

Imagine you have a writing practice.

Yes, coming to your craft consistently takes routine. Yes, creative writing rubs up against deeper fears of expression. However, when you allow yourself to step into being a writer, make space for the creativity, and make a plan to develop your own tailored practice, your writing skills will flourish.

Over the years, writers within the weekly Ideas Write Now workshop, following the same methodology from the writing practice outlined in this workbook, unearthed four by-products of this practice week after week.

- ▶ Writers spent less time overthinking or halted by pre-planning when challenged to write on a timer.
- ▶ Writers quieted their inner critic when challenged with endurance prompts.
- ▶ Writers grew comfortable in crafting a story arc in their first draft.
- ▶ Writers developed confidence in their artistic voice when given the space to read their work out loud.

Scan the QR code to join our next workshop!

How To Use This Workbook As A Writing Practice

The following pages are my writing practice on loan. This workbook contains 52 individual writing exercises ranging from 20-30 minutes per exercise. You can set this for a daily practice or break the 52 into a weekly practice. Each exercise is self-contained and follows a theme. Prompts to challenge you to write across a range of genres and styles. As the creative spirit you are, you can engage in these exercises in any order and on a schedule that suits your lifestyle. Write, incorporating the following exercises at the beginning of your writing practice, on a schedule that reflects your life.

The components of each exercise help you flex your creative muscles while offering writing strategies you can replicate as you build your writing practice. Each exercise utilizes the boundaries of timed writing and contains the following attributes:

- A writing introduction to offer motivation in moving forward with your craft
- A reminder to set an intention to guide your practice
- A physical ritual to train your mind and body for writing
- A warm-up to transition into a state of writing
- Compounding writing exercises to minimize anxiety about the blank page
- An endurance writing prompt to build writing stamina
- Guiding questions to stir the imagination

What Is A Writing Intention?

Some writing advice suggests writing daily; however, writing to check a box is a surefire way to burn out on passion. Writing to check a box is what rote memorization is to education—you're technically learning, but it's not sustainable long term. You aren't developing skills, you're satisfying the ego to write. Instead of thinking about writing in terms of meeting a daily quota, set an intention for your writing. Give yourself a reason to write, a purpose to put pen to paper or fingers to the keyboard. Setting an intention for writing gives you something to work toward in small steps while also sharpening your craft. Shifting from checking a box to exploring your craft affords you a growth mindset in your work.

Examples:

- I will incorporate new vocabulary into my work today.
- I will write from a new perspective.
- I will write in an unfamiliar style because I want to play.
- I will enter into a story without knowing the ending.
- I want to write with more imagination.
- I will write a story where dear Pickles, the pet poodle, makes an appearance.

What Is A Writing Ritual?

Less woo-woo than it sounds, a writing ritual is a way to step into writing. With busy lives and hundreds of distractions, writing requires focus, something you need to architect as a writer. A writing ritual trains your body, over time, to be prepared to write. As writing is a full-body experience, consider a physical ritual such as breathing, stretching, dancing, walking, or stepping into your writing space as a way to signal to your body that it's writing time. Back up your physical writing ritual with an easy mental ritual, such as a warm-up prompt, journal entry, haiku, or other stand-alone writing activity to get words on the page. The writing rituals outlined in this workbook combine a physical activity with a warm-up. Having a consistent writing ritual gets you into the flow state faster while also maximizing any time you can squeeze in for writing.

What Is Endurance Writing?

Endurance writing is a continuous state of production for a set amount of time. Writing in a continuous flow, overcoming awkward ideas, sentences, words, and images, breaks down the barriers of the ego. Endurance writing over time binds a stronger connection between bright ideas in your head and the words on the page. A fifteen-minute block of time eliminates the expectation of perfection. Removing the barrier of perfection works against the fear of writing something incorrectly. You can instead aim for a goal of continuous thought and production within a set time. The need for perfection is replaced with the satisfaction of having created. Having filled a blank page through pen to paper scribbling so fast you can hardly read the words. This style of writing, endurance writing, allows you to flex your writing muscles to build writing stamina.

Trigger Warning

Writing isn't created in a vacuum. To write, to create without acknowledging the complexities of being human, is a recipe for inauthenticity. There are themes within this workbook that might be triggering and also not suitable for children. Themes acknowledging the existence of sex, drugs, violence, mental health struggles, and death. You have the free will to skip any themes that might be a trigger.
Though I hope, as creators have done for centuries, you might use the page as a way to dive into areas of discomfort. Remember, it's your writing practice. The ideas to follow are creative kindling.

Home

The train runs the seafloor
between cities.
A window of blushing clouds.
Cracked buildings,
satellites salute.
We move
uptown, down to the marina & around the boats,
side streets to the medina.
Pretty, shiny textiles shadow
footsteps on the cobblestone causeway.
Follow the daisies to Pink Floyd—
Yassir's place.
USA tucked under his shirt:
1982, 1994, twenty-four, forty-three—calculations
through three languages of missing teeth.
A one-stop shop.
Three-syllable
sweets dissolve on your tongue
for a half dollar.
American?
Red bones, white thread, blue eyes—
How did you know?
Home, a place where the key sleeps,
your birth name tattooed on the mail.
From everywhere and nowhere,
echoed in a memory.
Texas?
Pocket my corrections.
A settlement—sedentary—
a place not my place, but
one as good as any.
Tea tight on my lips,
a nod, electric grin, a part to play.
Home.
Somewhere like that.

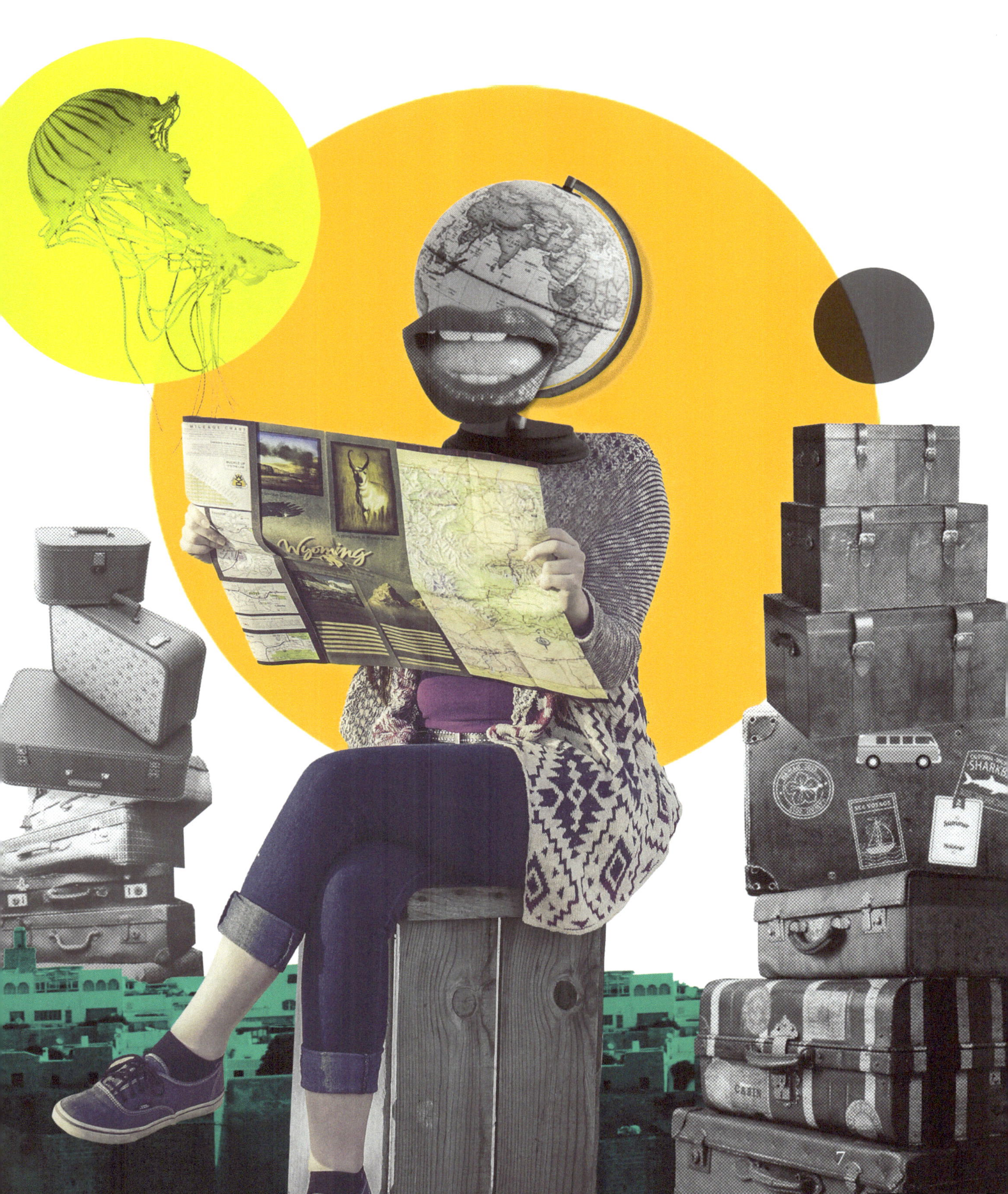

Wyoming

Persuasion

How do I convince you to pick up the pen? Do I lean into your desire to complete the project you've been daydreaming about for years, the one waiting for you? Do I validate your extraordinary voice, your creative prowess, your resilience? Maybe I remind you that your story begins with one word, one breadcrumb, following another. Perhaps I outline the yellow brick road of taking thought down the path to completion. No matter where I begin to stir the idea, there are three rhetorical tools necessary to deliver the best persuasive argument.

The ancient Greek philosopher, Aristotle, named these tools ethos, pathos, and logos. Aristotle championed the idea of effective communication as the trifecta of ethos, pathos, and logos. When blended, the cocktail of persuasion is intoxicating, smooth, irresistible, as displayed in speeches like Dr. Martin Luther King's "I Have A Dream" or in Charlton Heston's "America's First Freedom." However, when the components are missing, persuasion bounces rather than sticks. When we write persuasively, we work to avoid our readers walking away soured by poorly padded opinions on the page. We can learn from great speech writers like Clarence B. Jones and Helene Lange, essayists like Susan Lee Sontag and Langston Hughes, and philosophers like Simone de Beauvoir and Immanuel Kant, who have long elicited great thought through their rhetorical writing—the art of persuasive writing.

We come to the page with ideas informed by our opinions. We can choose how to shape ideas for the reader. We can choose our truth. We can help our audience burn with our truth kindled by reason, credibility, and feeling, to strike a match to the page.

In today's exercise, let's flex our persuasive muscles using opinion to paint a picture our audience can agree with.

Definitions:

▶ Ethos: credibility and ethics
▶ Pathos: emotions and feeling
▶ Logos: logic and reason

Set Your Intention For Today's Writing Practice

Your Writing Ritual:

▶ Stand or place your feet flat on the floor.
▶ Gently roll your head down across your chest.
▶ Circle your head back along your shoulders.
▶ Draw in a breath through your nose and breathe out through your mouth.
▶ Reverse the direction of your head roll.
▶ Repeat four times in each direction.

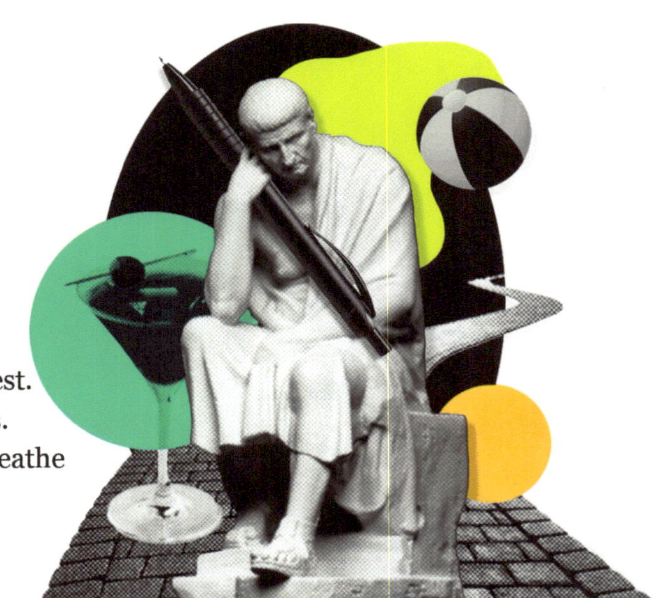

Set your timer for 2 mins.
Answer the following question.
When was the last time you had to persuade someone to agree with you?

Activity One:

Set your timer for 2 mins.
Jot down hot-button topics or ideas that garner different opinions based on the individual.
Examples: Do you believe in God? / Does pineapple belong on pizza? / Should you read more than one book at a time? / Is the Earth flat?

Activity Two:

Choose one hot-button topic from [Activity One].

Activity Three:

Set your timer for 1 min.
In relation to your idea picked in [Activity Two], what is your opinion about this hot-button topic?
Refine your opinion to two or three sentences.

Activity Four:

Set your timer for 1 min.
What is an opposing opinion to [Activity Three] laid out in two or three sentences?

Activity Five:

Set your timer for 5 mins.
What is your credibility to offer this opinion (ethos)?
What is the logic behind your opinion (logos)?
Why does this opinion ring true for you (pathos)?

Endurance Writing Prompt:
Set your timer for 10 mins.
Create an op-ed piece that begins with your clear position on a hot button topic [Activity Three]. Aim to persuade the reader to side with your opinion. Use ethos, logos, and pathos [Activity Five]. Make sure to address the opposing position to your opinion [Activity Four]. Wrap up with how you want the reader to feel about your opinion.

Guiding Questions:
What is at stake if others don't agree with your opinion?
How does your opinion offer a solution to a bigger question about life?

Lamp Light Dreamers

As is the spice of writing, we can amplify mundane aspects of our stories into fantastical scenes using personification. In "Falling Up," a poem by Shel Silverstein, the incessant, yet trivial thoughts plaguing sleep in the late hours of the night transform into creatures with the ability to crawl, creep, and party all night long in our heads. The creativity to move from simple (a thought) to the fantastical (a thought with arms and legs to bore into our ears) happens under the stencil of personification. What happens if, however, you invert personification in your writing?

As Charles Dickens shows us, inverted personification allows more dimension to people in fewer words. In several of his novels, he reverses the mechanics of personification. He paints his characters in light of their inanimate qualities: orphans as stocks and shares, people as tugboats, and the law as a scarecrow of a suit. He deploys inverted personification to vivify his descriptions. The monotonous humdrum of dinner party guests, as decorative, stagnant, polished, and positioned furniture, paints a powerful image.

Personification breathes life through a conch shell or the tassels of a carpet, while inverted personification reduces the animation of a being. Both allow the writer to intensify attributes where readers see characteristics over aesthetics.

In today's exercise, let's explore inverted personification to amplify characters in fewer words.

Definitions:
- Inverted (reverse) personification: when a non-human trait is attributed to a human.

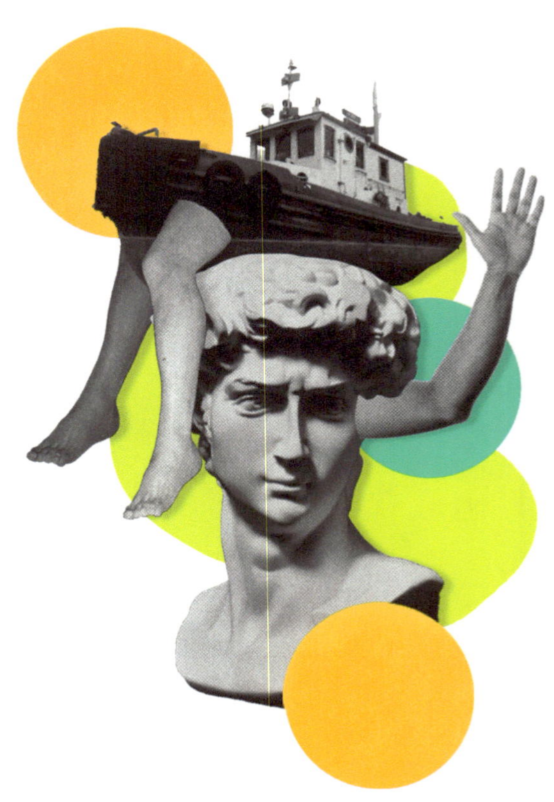

Set Your Intention For Today's Writing Practice

Your Writing Ritual:

- Stand or place your feet flat on the floor from a seated position.
- Close your eyes.
- Draw in a breath through your nose as you raise your arms above your head.
- Hold.
- Let out your breath in a sigh while dropping your arms down to the floor.
- Repeat this cycle six times.

Ideas come when we learn to let go.

Your Warm-Up:

Set your timer for 2 mins.
Answer the following question.
What parallels can you draw between how you feel and the inanimate objects in your space?

Activity One:

Set your timer for 2 mins.
Make a list of ways you could group people together. Examples: mothers / ballerinas / toddlers / astronauts

Activity Two:

Choose one group from [Activity One].

Activity Three:

Set your timer for 3 mins.
For the group picked in [Activity Two], make a list of attributes for someone who might be in this group.
Examples for ballerinas: angular / flexible / swift / majestic

Activity Four:

Set your timer for 2 mins.
Building on [Activity Three], jot down ideas on how someone from this group might contribute to society.
Examples for ballerinas: entertain / uphold high art / translate musical language into body language
/ keep people healthy

Activity Five:

Set your timer for 2 mins.
Make a list of non-human things that come to mind, matching one or many of your listed attributes from
[Activities Three and Four]. Examples: for ballerinas / a rainbow pinwheel / ribbon tethered to a tree limb
/ a bending straw / folded origami paper

Endurance Writing Prompt:

Set your timer for 15 mins.
Forget about coherence or a story and focus on descriptions. Create a snapshot of your type of person
from [Activity Two] and their place in society [Activity Three] using inverted personification. Paint
the picture and feeling by highlighting their non-human traits [Activity Five]. Be bold, declarative,
and avoid the use of like or as.

Guiding Questions:

What if you set your snapshot in a place your type of person would be uncomfortable?
How can you use sensory descriptions (five senses) around their nonhuman traits to show us
discomfort, joy, anger, etc?

Isolation

In fiction, confinement is a way to pressure our characters toward reverence. Characters like Winston from *1984* in Room 101, the Captain in *The Sympathizer*, and the woman in "The Yellow Wallpaper," exemplify the fragility of sanity when characters endure solitude against their will. The fear of being left to our minds time and again play a role in fiction.

Two paths of narrative plot divert from the setting of confinement. One plot is where the character dives deeply inward *(The Sympathizer, 1984, One Flew Over The Cuckoo's Nest)*, or the second plot is where the character expands outward, exploring, inch by inch, the setting of their confined world ("The Yellow Wallpaper," *The Memory Police*). In either, we get a microscopic view of the human condition when confined to restrictive spaces, when left to ourselves. We are intrigued by the psychological duality of being in control of and controlled by our minds.

We, as the reader, are asked to endeavor to follow the madness of humans thinking about thinking, rethinking about thought, overanalyzing purpose, worth, devotion, identity, and meaning. At the last turn of the page, with privilege, most of us can return to a life where the door is unlocked and the windows are free of bars.

However, in 2021, society was asked to shelter in place. The world shut down. Many were experiencing isolation and confinement for the first time, discovering, whether intentional or not, "that the ultimate life-and-death struggle is with ourselves. Foreign invaders might kill (your) body, but only (you) could kill (your) spirit."[42]

In today's exercise, just as an author would use a confined space to amplify feeling and narrow in on a character, let's use experiences from the pandemic as reflection in our creative writing.

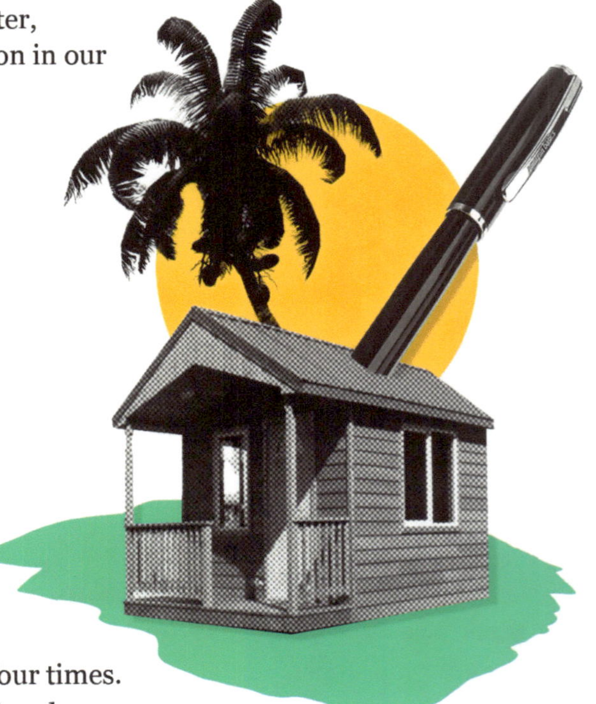

Set Your Intention For Today's Writing Practice

Your Writing Ritual:

- ► Stand or place your feet flat on the floor.
- ► Extend your left arm up to the sky.
- ► Extend your right arm down toward the floor.
- ► Lengthen your reach by wiggling your fingers.
- ► Switch arms on each inhale, repeating the cycle four times.
- ► Drop your arms to your side and shake out your hands.

Your Warm-Up:

Set your timer for 2 mins.

Answer the following question.

What is one thing you discovered about yourself during COVID you wouldn't have otherwise known?

Activity One:

Set your timer for 2 mins.

Make a list of "what" questions that someone might ponder if quarantined for an extended period.
Examples: What hygiene habits have gone out the window? / What can I live without? / What can't I live without? / What meals can I make with ramen noodles and Heinz ketchup?

Activity Two:

Set your timer for 30 seconds.

Where did you spend 95% of your time during the pandemic? Examples: family room couch
/ treehouse / bathroom for privacy / garage

Activity Three:

Choose a space from [Activity Two].

Activity Four:

Set your timer for 2 mins.

Make a list of details about the space where you spent 95% of your time during the pandemic.
Examples: smattered bird poop on the west window / bugs buzzing / the squish of the shag rug
/ the muffled theme music of movies playing in the adjacent room

Activity Five:

Set your timer for 1 min.

Choose one identifier to describe who you were during the pandemic. Examples: gassy / annoyed
/ loopy / cabin crazed

Endurance Writing Prompt:

Set your timer for 15 mins.

You have been tasked to document your experience during COVID-19 by writing a short exposé about your space [Activity Three]. Use questions from [Activity One] to unpack your feelings about sheltering in place. Use descriptions from [Activity Four] to set the scene. Challenge yourself to use the following format to begin your exposé. I am (name)__________. I am (identifier)__________. I have been sheltering-in-place for (#)____ days.

Guiding Questions:

Why did you choose the specific space you spent 95% of your time in during the pandemic?
What did you see, as if for the first time, in this space?

Can O' Beans

Strange as it may be to think your couch or your kitchen table has perspective, writers have long used inanimate objects to tell stories. My favorite example is in the novel *Skinny Legs and All*. Author Tom Robbins tells the story of a woman seeking artistic freedom as her partner continues to gain artistic recognition. In her journey, she loses precious objects along the way, and Robbins blends the landscape of possibility as these inanimate objects (Can o' Beans, Dirty Sock, Spoon, Painted Stick, and Conch Shell) play key roles in unmasking the pain, pleasure, and freedom of lifting the veils of society.

Personifying inanimate objects allows you, as the writer, to broach subjects and taboos with a wider lens, detached from the assumptions and biases the reader brings to your work.

In today's exercise, let's personify the objects around us to view the world from a different perspective.

Definitions:

▶ Personification: the attribution of a personal nature or human characteristics to something non-human, or the representation of an abstract quality in human form.

▶ Third-person omniscient narrator: an all-knowing narrator, "godlike" or deliberately "authorial" persona that allows an author to comment on the action with the benefit of distance.

Set Your Intention For Today's Writing Practice

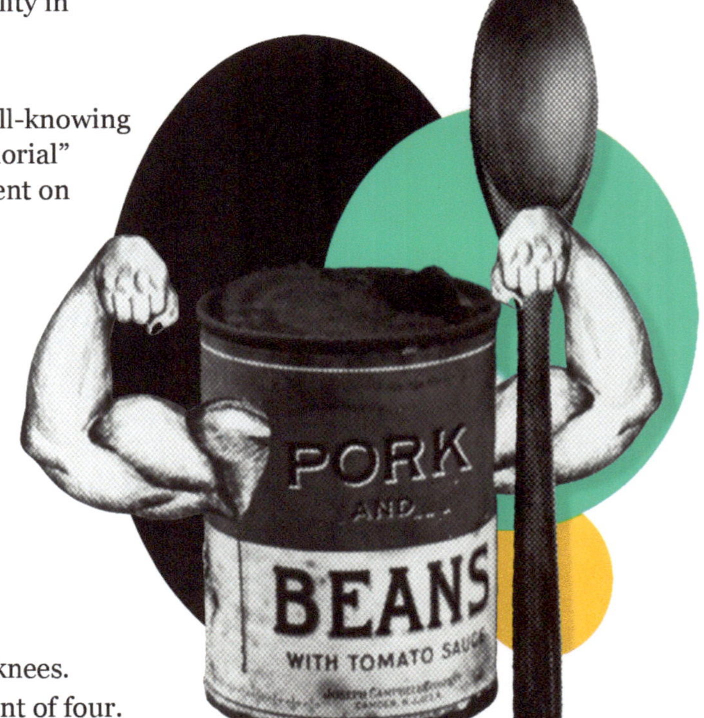

Your Writing Ritual:

▶ Sit and place your feet flat on the floor.
▶ Lay your hands, palm-side up, on your knees.
▶ Breathe in through your nose to the count of four.
▶ Breathe out through your mouth to the count of five.
▶ For each breath in, focus on the palms of your hands.
▶ Repeat your breathing cycle until you feel a warmth starting in your hands.

Your Warm-Up:

Set your timer for 2 mins.
Answer the following question.
If the couch or chair you're sitting on could speak, what would it say right now?

Activity One:

Set your timer for 2 mins.
Make a list of objects within your view. Examples: pen / clown nose / dying desk plant / postcard

Activity Two:

Choose one item from [Activity One] to personify.

Activity Three:

Set your timer for 2 mins.
Make a list of all the things an object might see or experience during the day. Examples for a postcard:
from the market, watching people pass by / handled and stuffed in a bag / slammed on the counter face down
 / licked and slapped with a stamp

Activity Four:

Set your timer for 2 mins.
Make a list of questions that your object might have about existence if it suddenly became self-aware.
Examples for a postcard: What is love? / What is the meaning of life? / What is worship? / Why is there
smoke?

Activity Five:

Choose one question from [Activity Four].

Endurance Writing Prompt:
Set your timer for 15 mins.
Create a third-person omniscient narrative about the life of your object [Activity Two]. Imagine they
have thoughts, feelings, and curiosities about the world and move from this idea as fact. Jump into a
scene where your object is experiencing the world [Activity Three] and in search of answering one
specific question [Activity Five].

Guiding Questions:
How does your object feel about the world they are experiencing?
What quest might help them find the answer to their burning question?

A Box Of Rocks

My body language radiated *leave me alone* as I nestled into a spot at the coffee shop. At the adjacent table, a man in his fifties waved in my direction to garner my attention. I lost track of my sentence on the page. He had two USPS boxes next to his laptop and a strange digital microscope. He waved and pointed at his boxes. I smiled, annoyed, gearing up excuses to shut down our conversation after whatever question he invariably needed to ask. Carl, we'll call him, was looking for an audience. Carl wanted to show me his rocks. He carefully pulled one rock out onto the coffee table. He had a microscope he used to project the image onto his computer. He motioned for me to look.

I thought about Tom Hanks in the moment. Hanks said in an interview on writing, that storytelling draws life from your interaction with the world.[20] He cautions that we're in an age of flowing through life plugged in, deaf to the beat of the world around us. I could deafen out Carl and his box of rocks.

I pulled out my earbuds instead. I gave in. Carl was looking for gold, specs hidden in the broken sheets of sedimentary rocks he had shipped from his land deep in the mountains. We spent the next forty-five minutes talking about minerals, his ailing father, bologna sandwiches, the changes in the neighborhood and his hopes to be rich. Carl sits at the coffee shop every day making new friends and finding connections—whether people welcome him or not. I came to enjoy his persistence.

As Hanks suggests, if you tune in, if you're present and aware, stories will find you. If you want to write with truth, engage with strangers. Be open to conversation. Seek new perspectives on the world.

In today's exercise, let's reflect on encounters with strangers having made ripples in your perspective on the human experience.

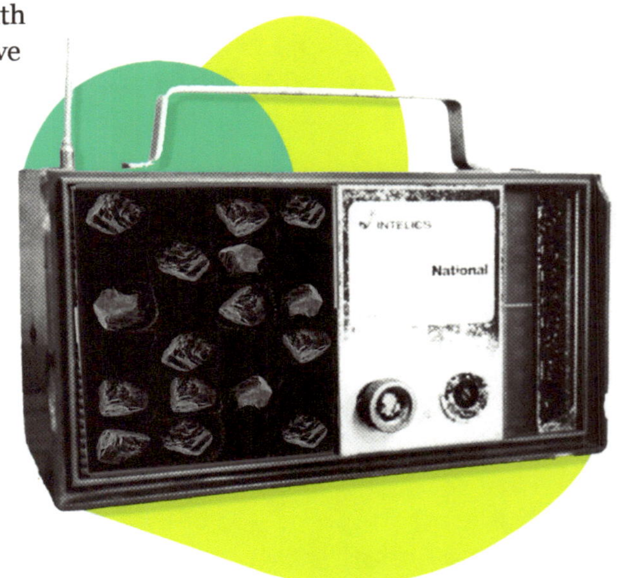

Set Your Intention For Today's Writing Practice

Your Writing Ritual:
- Stand with your feet slightly apart.
- Shake out your hands for five seconds.
- Inhale deeply and reach both arms up.
- Exhale and fold forward, letting your arms dangle.
- Sway gently side to side for three breaths.
- Slowly roll up to standing.

Set your timer for 2 mins.
Answer the following question.
How do you pick your seat in public spaces?

Set your timer for 2 mins.
Jot down a list of times you might interact with a stranger. Examples: in line at the bank / at the library / stuck in a traffic jam / the circus

Set your timer for 2 mins.
Reflect on the last couple weeks to make a list of encounters you've had with a stranger. Examples: parking attendant shouting his love for the USA with two thumbs up / Jack, the silver-fox lumber jack librarian / the retired writing teacher volunteering at the library / Kristen, the grant writer in the elevator

Choose one specific encounter from [Activity Two].

Set your timer for 2 mins.
Jot down a list of words to describe the encounter. Examples: uncomfortable / enlightening / noncommittal / sticky

Endurance Writing Prompt:
Set your timer for 15 mins.
Write a journal entry pulling apart a recent chance encounter with a stranger [Activity Three].
Give us the context and setting. Bring us right into the interaction, positive or negative, you had with a stranger. Use words from [Activity Four] to dissect how you felt about the experience and what you might have learned from the encounter.

Guiding Questions:
If you met this stranger again, what would you say?
What did your body language communicate beyond what your words said?

What Fluffy Thinks

Working from home, my dogs are my greatest company. I work through writing ideas in dialogue with my pups—Tocineta and Chicharrón. I ask them questions or make rhetorical remarks. A head tilt or a long exhale is all I need to confirm a good idea. I am constantly talking to them, playing both sides of the conversation. I like to interpret their moves, a paw at my feet, a lick of the cheek, as his way of contributing to our conversation, but of course, we're never 100% on the same page. I wish sometimes they were more of a muse than amused. It's like, as John Steinbeck writes in his memoir about traveling across America with his dog Charley, "I've seen a look in dogs' eyes, a quickly vanishing look of amazed contempt, and I am convinced that dogs think humans are nuts."[57]

If my dogs could speak, what would they say? How might they call me out on my slack, console me when upset, compliment me on a well-placed metaphor, or persuade me to take them on more walks?

Phillip Pullman, author of the trilogy *His Dark Materials*, plays out the idea of animals as both muse and companion in his work. His daemons in the parallel universes that Lily and Will explore are physical manifestations of the soul. Daemons have the power of speech and thought, with an overlay of animal capabilities. In other words, daemons are the pets we wish we had.

Pullman and Steinbeck remind us that creative writing is a way to step into the mind of characters or to explore the world from unexpected viewpoints. A reminder that creativity has no bounds and every living thing can be a new perspective in your writing.

In today's exercise, let's explore fictional writing where animals of the world have the capacity to communicate in language we understand.

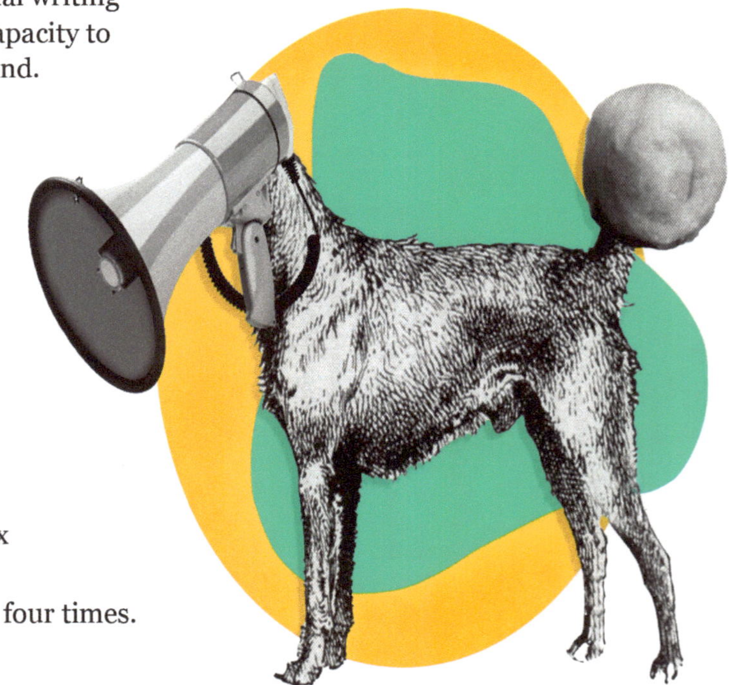

Set Your Intention For Today's Writing Practice

Your Writing Ritual:

► Stand or sit comfortably.
► Place your hands behind your back and clasp them gently.
► Inhale through your nose and draw your shoulder blades together.
► Exhale through your mouth and relax your arms.
► Repeat the movement and breathing four times.
► Shake out your hands.

Your Warm-Up:

Set your timer for 2 mins.
Answer the following question.
If you could be an animal, what animal suits you?

Activity One:

Set your timer for 2 mins.
Jot down a list of words, phrases, thoughts a pet might have if they could talk. Examples: food, food, food / Now? Can we go on a walk now? Now? / I'll eat that. / You expect me to come to you? No, no, you can come to me.

Activity Two:

Set your timer for 2 mins.
Make a list of pet names. Examples: Mr. Squirt / Titan / Muffin / Turtle

Activity Three:

Set your timer for 2 mins.
Make a list of questions someone might wish their pets could answer if they could talk. Examples: How do I get you to take a dump faster? / How exactly do you know he's a bad man? / What are you singing about? / Why are you looking at me like that?

Activity Four:

Choose a pet name from [Activity Two].

Activity Five:

Choose a question from [Activity Three].

Endurance Writing Prompt:

Set your timer for 15 mins.
A humane study is being conducted on animals as scientists test collars that have the ability to compute brain waves into human language. They're monitoring you and your pet [Activity Four] in your natural habitat at home. They are running tests on answering the question of [Activity Five]? Drop us into a scene of you in your natural habitat hearing your pet speak for the first time in language you can understand.

Guiding Questions:

How does your body language affect what your pet says?
Beyond the study, what is something you've been dying to get your pet's perspective on?

The Weight Of A Word

A word can be twisted and taken, both given and withheld. Something that in one light is sacred and in its shadow is profane. Words can be pitted as a weapon and explored like they have a lid. Something everyone can hold and that needs breath to live. Or as Viet Than Nguyen aptly states in *The Sympathizer*, "I was writing to a writer who valued the force of a sentence and the weight of a word."[43] A writer has both the punch and the duty to wield words well.

Part of showing and not telling in your writing is your use of words. As a writer, you can liberate ideas through word choice. You can behold truth or fidget with meaning. You can karate kick your reader's sense of place and thought. Writing well is a practice of wielding the scalpel against malignant language burrowed in your prose.

In today's exercise, let's explore a disruption in plain language to show in our writing.

Definition:

► Passive voice: a form or set of forms of a verb in which the subject undergoes the action of the verb (e.g. they were killed as opposed to the active form he killed them). If you can add the phrase "by zombies" to the end of your sentence and it makes sense, then you've likely used passive voice.

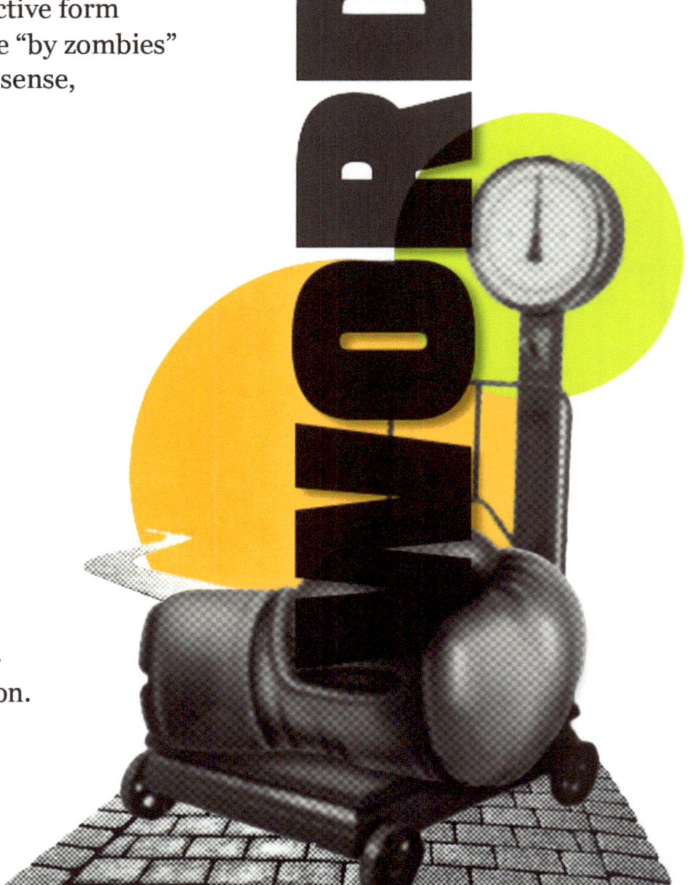

Set Your Intention For Today's Writing Practice

Your Writing Ritual:

► Stand or sit with your arms at your sides.
► Inhale and roll your wrists in one direction.
► Exhale and reverse the roll.
► Keep the movement slow and connected to your breath.
► Repeat for four breath cycles.
► Shake out your hands.

Your Warm-Up:

Set your timer for 2 mins.
Answer the following question.
How do you tell a stranger about your day versus telling a loved one?

Activity One:

Set your timer for 1 min.
Jot down a list of verbs or phrases that come to mind when you hear the word afraid. Examples: darkness
/ vomit / falling / chills

Activity Two:

Set your timer for 1 min.
Jot down a list of verbs or phrases that come to mind when you hear the word happy. Examples: jitters / wiggle
/ vibrant / music

Activity Three:

Set your timer for 1 min.
Jot down a list of verbs or phrases that come to mind when you hear the word sad. Examples: heavy
/ hollow / rain / soup

Activity Four:

Choose a state of being from [Activities One - Three]: afraid, happy, or sad.

Activity Five:

Set your timer for 5 mins.
Rewrite the line, I feel [Activity Four]. Add examples from your previous list to create an image of the feeling.

Activity Six:

Set your timer for 2 mins.
Review what you wrote in [Activity Five]. Circle anywhere you used the passive voice in your writing.

Endurance Writing Prompt:

Set your timer for 10 mins.
Rewrite the passage using active language. Expand on the feeling using elevated verbs and phrases
from your list. Inhabit the action in your story. Show us feeling like it's a scene painted across the
inside of our eyelids.

Guiding Questions:

How can you reimagine the theme using your senses?
Why does this feeling resonate with you?

Sweaty Palms

In a workshop in Casablanca, a friend requested we write scary stories. With excitement, I set to shape our next workshop around the topic. The cursor on the page flickered minute after minute as I came to the sour realization of having little inspiration of my own to guide us. I turned to the spookiest story I know, *The Shining*.

The novel follows the Torrance family isolated deep in the Rocky Mountains of Colorado after Jack accepts a position as a caretaker for the Stanley Hotel over the winter. Chapter after chapter, Stephen King peels back the hauntings of the hotel. Danny, Jack and Wendy's five-year-old son, endures distressing illusions as the days go by: the firehose as a snake, an invisible creature in the snow, the ghost party in the elevator. Simmering underneath Danny's supposed nightmares, Jack is slowly losing his mind.

King continues to scare us by igniting a series of petrifying thoughts. What if you lost control of your reality? What if you couldn't distinguish what was tangible and what was imagined? Who would you trust?

More than the ghosts, Jack's plummet toward insanity strikes terror in the reader. Monsters, aliens, or murderers, in art, exist outside the individual and therefore can be destroyed to some degree. However, to destroy insanity would be to destroy oneself—a thought that makes for an unnerving story.

King creates an eerie novel by doubling down on the plot of an unhinged mind. The loss of sanity is chilling to a wider audience. Creating a scary story, then begins by exploring collective fear.

In your writing, when you can zero in on aspects of human nature down to their simplest form, like the fear of the unknown, fear of losing control, fear of insanity, your writing takes on a familiarity for the reader, one they are compelled to follow, even if shaking in their seats.

In today's exercise, let's craft a scary story by exploiting our reader's fear of the unknown.

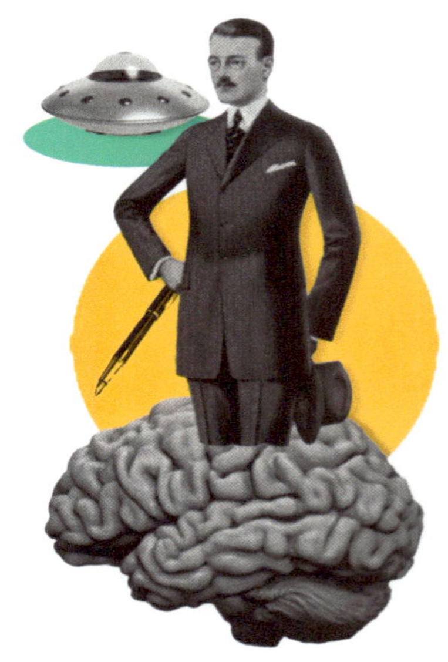

Set Your Intention For Today's Writing Practice

Your Writing Ritual:

► Sit comfortably and close your eyes.
► Inhale and imagine drawing energy up from your feet.
► Exhale and send that energy out through your fingertips.
► Repeat the visualization with each breath for five cycles.
► Open your eyes and wiggle your fingers.
► Stretch your arms out wide, then release.

Set your timer for 2 mins.
Answer the following question.
Where does your belief or disbelief in ghosts come from?

Activity One:
Set your timer for 2 mins.
Tap into your five senses and create a list that paints a picture of what being afraid looks like and feels like.
Examples: quickened breath / grinding teeth / tense shoulders / profuse foul language

Activity Two:
Set your timer for 2 mins.
Make a list of suspenseful elements in a scary story. Examples: knocking noise / shadow at the end of a dark road /creaking floors in an empty house / a raging storm

Activity Three:
Set your timer for 2 mins.
Make a list of plot twists in a scary story. Examples: the narrator is a ghost / the house is haunted / the child is possessed / the protagonist's soul is trapped in a mirror

Activity Four:
Choose a plot twist from [Activity Three].

Endurance Writing Prompt:
Set your timer for 15 mins.
As a first-person narrator, open up your scary story with a suspenseful element [Activity Two]. Jump into the fear and anxiety of our narrator [Activity One]. Show us what's happening step by step, engaging in inner monologue leading to our inevitable plot twist [Activity Four].

Guiding Questions:
What has led the narrator to this moment of suspense?
How is your narrator interacting with other characters or are they entirely alone?

To The Water

In the spring of 2023, my father passed away after a short battle with pancreatic cancer. I was in the middle of putting together this workbook when life pulled me in a varied direction. I grieved. I abandoned self-care. I couldn't define happiness. Water became a sense of therapy. I drew baths. I traveled to the ocean several times a week to cry with the sunset. I set background videos of the shore on my computer. I craved water. Submersion was a center, a space between physical pain and endurance. The weightlessness, in irony, kept me grounded.

In my return to creative writing, it was also water that revived me. After months of not writing, I took my journals and a laptop to a cafe overlooking the ocean. I metaphorically strapped myself to a chair. I forced myself to write, without agenda, to get to a more accepting practice. The self-inflicting criticism was brutal. I let everything find a place on the page. To my surprise, the ocean curved through segmented lines of that session. I fell into a transitive state staring at the ocean. My fingers danced. My creative brain took the wheel. I explored how many ways I could describe the same scene, the ocean, before me. The movement, the smell, the reminders, the triggers, the colors, the presence of power, all lured me into a stream of consciousness. Turning over and over the same horizon drew me closer to comfort. I was reminded of the patience we require in coming to writing. The acceptance we must allow if we want to get into a flow state.

In today's exercise, let's use the subject of water to buoy our patience and draw us closer to creative intuition.

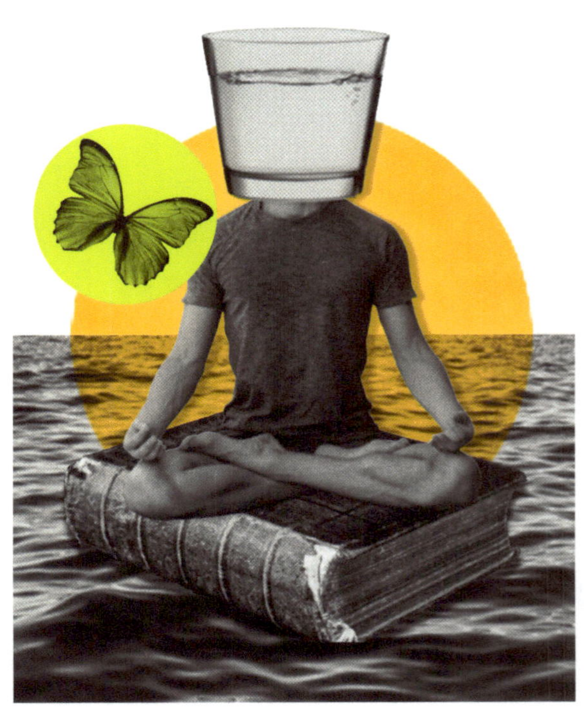

Set Your Intention For Today's Writing Practice

Your Writing Ritual:

- Stand or place your feet flat on the floor.
- Draw in your breath, expanding your chest fully.
- Hold your breath to the count of five.
- Exhale fully out of your mouth.
- Hold to the count of five.
- Repeat your breathing four times.

Your Warm-Up:

Set your timer for 2 mins.
Answer the following question.
How was the last time you took a plunge into water?

Activity One:

Set your timer for 2 mins.
Make a list of as many forms of water as you can think of. Examples: ocean / condensation / sparkling / streams

Activity Two:

Set your timer for 2 mins.
Make a list of verbs to describe what you can do with or in water. Examples: drink / play / resist / spray

Activity Three:

Set your timer for 2 mins.
Make a list of memories you can recall of having been submerged in water. Examples: held underwater in neighbors pool / floating in the river / caught walking in torrential rain in Vietnam / soaking in the tub

Endurance Writing Prompt:
Set your timer for 15 mins.
Your theme is water. Just as water forms to its container, use the space of the page to form your ideas on your relationship to water. Start zoomed out with all the ways water appears in the world [Activity One]. Draw closer by examining its purpose and movement in the world [Activity Two]. Zoom in on the specifics of water memories from your life [Activity Three].

Guiding Questions:
When was a time you felt the raw power of water?
What are three memorable events in your life where water played a central role?

Fairy Godly Advice

Neil Gaiman has a short story called "October Tale" that has stuck with me. A genie is released from captivity within his lamp. We, as the reader, can assume where the story will go. Gaiman, however, finds a new path in a tale we know all too well. In "October Tale," the woman who is granted three wishes has no desires. She has no wants or wishes. The genie finds himself free with no wishes to grant. What then is his purpose?

Gaiman's clever storytelling and imagination take our characters on a tale of domestic life. The genie cannot seem to leave the woman's side. The woman stays true to her lack of want and desire while the genie softens to a world of domesticity, a way of giving without expectation to do so.

Gaiman turns a trope inside out, shakes the fabric of an age-old narrative, and pins the finely washed new story on the clothesline to dry. I love this story because it's a reminder of how writing is open to endless possibilities. We can architect a new story with the fine dust of old tales. *Wicked* is another example. The wicked witch is given the spotlight to shake out her side of the story. *The True Story Of The Three Little Pigs*, yet another example. The wolf, as our narrator, flips our perception of a classic on its head.

As a writer, you can mold stories from all kinds of ideas. You can draw inspiration from stories past and present, tooling your take on what's been done.

In today's exercise, let's explore the classic tale of a wish-granting fairy godmother to play on new perspectives.

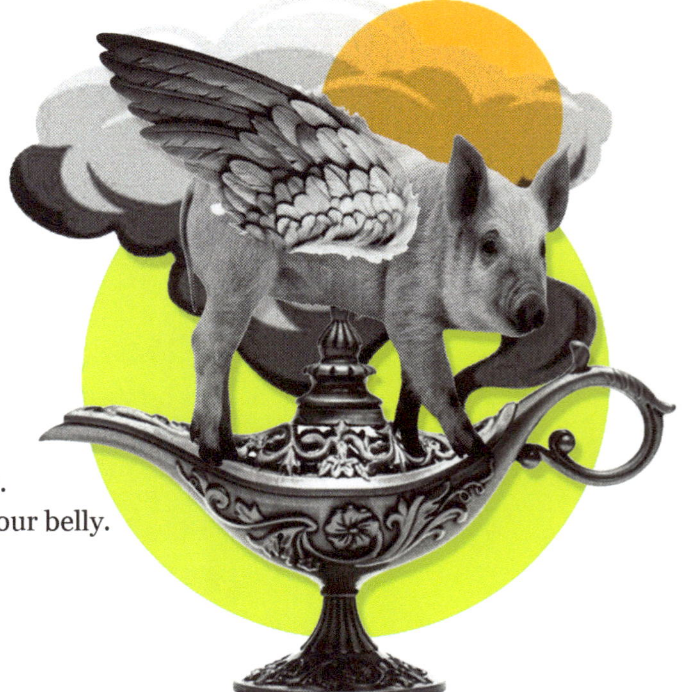

Set Your Intention For Today's Writing Practice

Your Writing Ritual:
- Sit or stand with your feet flat on the floor.
- Rest one hand on your heart and one on your belly.
- Breathe in slowly through your nose, feeling both hands rise.
- Exhale gently through your mouth, feeling your body soften.
- Repeat this breath cycle five times.
- Drop your hands to your side and shake them out.

Set your timer for 2 mins.
Answer the following question.
How would you imagine your personal fairy godmother might look?

Activity One:
Set your timer for 2 mins.
Make a list of what a fairy godmother usually does when crisis strikes in a story. Examples: save the maiden from a poor choice / withholds the all knowing answer / fixes the problem with their wand / offers unsolicited advice

Activity Two:
Set your timer for 2 mins.
Make a list of absurd responses for a fairy godmother in a crisis. Examples: light up a cigarette / tell the protagonist they're screwed / tidying up the place / teaching physics

Activity Three:
Choose an absurdity from [Activity Two].

Activity Four:
Set your timer for 2 mins.
What are everyday modern troubles someone might want to call in backup to tackle? Examples: defusing conflict at work / bullies at school / bangs or no bangs / going through heartbreak

Activity Five:
Choose an everyday trouble from [Activity Four].

Endurance Writing Prompt:
Set your timer for 15 mins.
A fairy godmother arrives on scene. Poof, your story begins as a character meets their godmother during a time of crisis [Activity Five]. Had this been a traditional tale, perhaps your fairy godmother would have a prompt and magical solution. Instead, they do something entirely different [Activity Three], breaking all expectations of how a fairy godmother should behave. Jump into the action.

Guiding Questions:
What led your fairy godmother to such a different approach to her magical role?
How does your character engage with their fairy godmother's odd response to their crisis?

The Neighborhood

Amelie and her husband, Jorge, regaled details about their lives as travelers often do when they meet for the first time in a new place, sitting side by side at a restaurant. Within minutes, I knew the most minute details about their lives down to the preference of how their Labrador plays in the dog park at home in New York City.

In the curvature of the conversation, Amelia shared that they both were in the parking lot of the Twin Towers when the first plane hit, September 11th, 2001. Jorge recalled the windshield busted in his car from debris, the heat from the fire above as the two ran out into the street. He remembers the smell of the fuel, the eerie remark of a stranger in the street telling him he was white as a ghost. Amelia remembers the glass of the department store windows across the street vibrating with the unsteadiness of the towers. She said her mind tried to rationalize the movement being caused by the wind when she knew the air was still.

Amelia said if Jorge hadn't been hungover, making them late, she would have been on the 95th floor that morning. I allowed myself to feel the chills of their story. I wondered how we ended up on the subject as complete strangers. Will the world ever think of New York without tying the place to its tragedy? Perhaps for New Yorkers, it's an unavoidable piece of who they are, a broken bone forever aching when the temperature drops. The tragedy is a scar reminding them of exactly where they stood that day, who they called, what the air smelled like, and how close they came to death—even decades later.

As Amelie had shown me, where we're from is inescapable in telling our story. As writers, we can embrace or we can dilute our story through the lens of a place. Where we come from can turn out on the page, in our characters, in our settings, in our plot. You have roots. You have history. Writing well is a perpetual examination of your personal history to make sense of the world.

In today's exercise, let's use creative nonfiction to explore your story in relation to where you're from.

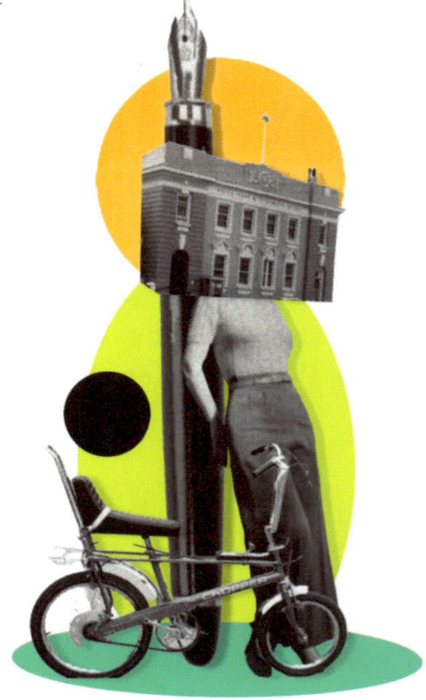

Set Your Intention For Today's Writing Practice

Your Writing Ritual:

▶ Stand with your feet hip-width apart.

▶ Inhale while reaching your right arm up and over your head.

▶ Exhale and return to center.

▶ Inhale and stretch your left arm up and over your head.

▶ Exhale and return.

▶ Repeat this flow four times on each side.

Set your timer for 2 mins.
Answer the following question.
Describe the room you are writing from today.

Activity One:
When people ask you where you're from, what is your answer?

Activity Two:
Set your timer for 2 mins.
Using the answer from [Activity One], create a list of details about where you're from. Examples: biggest hill in town littered by smashed pumpkins every October / the edge of the mountains / the waft of Coors Brewing hops in the air / safety

Activity Three:
Set your timer for 2 mins.
Building from the place in [Activity One], jot down ideas of how outsiders might have viewed where you're from or perhaps what the place is "known for." Examples: the Rad Arvada / active people everywhere / passive niceties / Columbine

Activity Four:
Set your timer for 2 mins.
Based on your place form [Activity One], what are some of the major events that happened in your life in this place? Examples: childhood, adolescence, off to college / first car, first kiss, first fuck / Gunther Tooties diner becomes the Spice Room

Endurance Writing Prompt:
Set your timer for 15 mins.
Create a snapshot of where you're from [Activity One]. Crack open your thoughts and give us a unique tour of where you're from [Activity Two]. If we were strangers to this place, how would outsiders think of where you're from [Activity Three]? Pull the snapshot together with your specific memories of the place [Activity Four].

Guiding Questions:
Where could you get the best food in this place?
How do you think you'd be different if you weren't from this place?

A Countable Crime

My first short story was a mystery I wrote for my third-grade class. I was under the influence of Lemony Snicket and enthralled with the Baudelaire children. I wrote mystery first, unknowingly, because it offered the greatest reward for my reader. I was drawn to the charm and challenge of a whodunit. In youth, life seems out of reach. We can't stay up past bedtime. We must always ask for permission. We are too short to ride amusement rides. However, regardless of limitations of age or situation, we can enter into a world of mystery and, with absolute authority, solve the case.

More heavily than in other genres, crime fiction calls on the reader to take part in the story. Since Edgar Allen Poe's work "The Murders in the Rue Morgue," detectives—Sherlock Holmes, The Hardy Boys, and Nancy Drew—have all brought us on board to get to the bottom of things.

The exchange between reader and author under the pretense of high-stakes mystery is a unique playground to create. You can pull the strings between conversations, drop statements, and turn suspicion to conjure plot in a way that demands the reader to follow.

One powerful narrative tool in the genre is fixing objects as anchors. A letter left behind, broken glass, blood splattered in a pattern suggesting blunt force trauma. Objects can both carry the mystery and lure you to revelation.

In today's exercise, let's explore crime fiction with objects as our breadcrumbs.

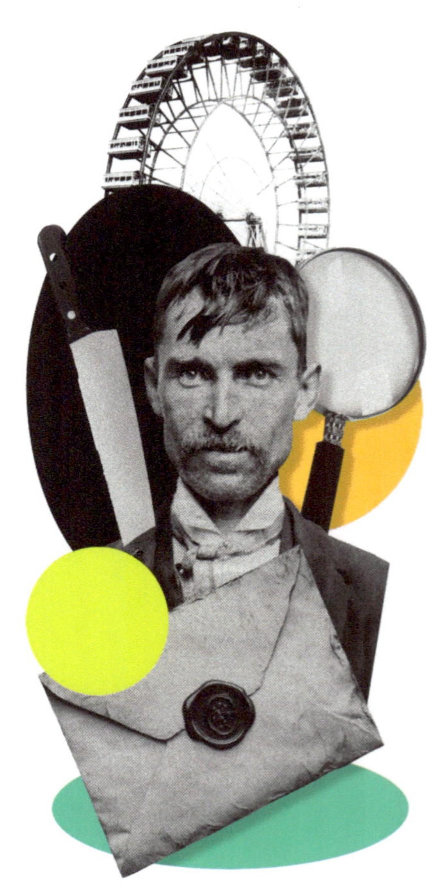

Set Your Intention For Today's Writing Practice

Your Writing Ritual:

► Stand or place your feet flat on the floor.
► Draw your breath in through your nose while bringing your arms to the sky.
► Slowly fold forward while exhaling and dropping your arms.
► Touching your toes, breathe in through your nose and out through your mouth.
► Repeat your breathing four times.
► Rise to an upright position and shake out your hands.

Set your timer for 2 mins.

Answer the following question.

What would be your best attribute if you were a detective?

Activity One:

Set your timer for 2 mins.

Make a list of the countable objects you can see. Examples: books / fallen rose petals / droplets of liquid / dust bunnies

Activity Two:

Ascribe a number to five of your countable objects from [Activity One]. Examples: 1 book / 8 fallen rose petals / 5 droplets of liquid / 9 dust bunnies

Activity Three:

Set your timer for 2 mins.

Make a list of crimes, mysteries, or cases a detective might be tasked to solve. Examples: Who stole the cookies? / Where is Charlie? / How did they steal the money? / Who murdered George?

Activity Four:

Choose a crime, mystery, or case from [Activity Three].

Endurance Writing Prompt:

Set your timer for 15 mins.

An unusual case unfolds, the case of the [Activity Four]. There are quite a few unknowns, shrouding the case in mystery, but we do know that a collection of objects is involved [Activity Two]. Jump into the case writing as either an omniscient narrator or first-person detective.

Guiding Questions:

Why is your detective perfect for the case?

How does your detective run through scenarios to make an educated guess as to solving the case?

All Grown Up

In *Lord of the Flies,* a group of boys stranded on an island must survive. They attempt to grow up all at once, fulfilling a fantasy of many children to govern themselves. Tension leads to emotional reaction over rational thought. They unconsciously form a hierarchy; their rules have no reason, their punishments cruel.

Coming away from the book depleted by Piggy's fate, I journaled about the moments in my childhood where, in a similar wish, I wanted to grow up, to govern myself. To abolish bedtime and homework. To nix all the vegetables from my plate and to ban long-legged adults from parades. The frustrations of childhood endlessly bumped up against "what was good for me." I was prevented from running wild in the park without a coat. Restrained from plummeting into the pool until my lunch had settled. Repeatedly, something just beyond my age, my allotted self-governance, my control, stoked the fire of frustration I wouldn't escape unless I could grow up.

Turns out that growing up isn't the key to escaping frustration. I still brush up against discomfort when my technology knows more than I do or when the to-do list spans longer than the hours. When I fail to say the right word or receive unsolicited advice. I would gladly return to the days of having an enforced bedtime.

That's the thing, isn't it? What's frustrating in the moment, with time and perspective, can shine with new meaning. Bedtime for an eight-year-old can be perceived as a punishment, whereas for a thirty-four-year-old, bedtime can be perceived as a boundary for self care. Frustration is still palpable whether you're eight, eighteen, twenty-eight, or eighty, but the meaning you draw from these moments shifts.

In today's exercise, let's use writing to explore perceived injustices from childhood by unpacking these moments with an adult lens.

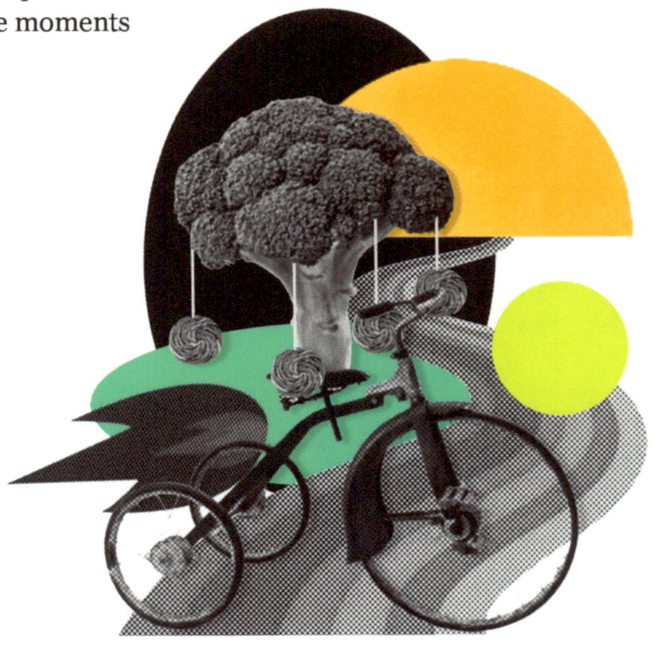

Set Your Intention For Today's Writing Practice

Your Writing Ritual:

- ▸ Sit with your spine straight and your feet grounded.
- ▸ Place your hands over your ribs.
- ▸ Inhale and feel your ribs expand.
- ▸ Exhale and feel them contract.
- ▸ Continue for five deep breaths.
- ▸ Release your hands and circle your wrists.

Your Warm-Up:
Set your timer for 2 mins.
Answer the following question.
What frustrates you about being an adult?

Activity One:
Set your timer for 2 mins.
Make a list of actions, reactions, or words a child might exhibit if they were frustrated. Examples: scream
/ pout / punch / draw on the wall

Activity Two:
Set your timer for 2 mins.
Make a list of actions, reactions, or words you exhibit when you're frustrated. Examples: clench your fists
/ swear / call your bestie and bitch / eat

Activity Three:
Set your timer for 2 mins.
Make a list of things you imagine or remember being frustrated with as a child (before age 13).
Examples: bedtime / being told what to do / having to eat vegetables before leaving the table
/ not being told the whole truth

Activity Four:
Choose a frustration from [Activity Three] that triggers a specific memory.

Endurance Writing Prompt:
Set your timer for 15 mins.
Journal about a memory where you were frustrated as a child, specific to what you chose in [Activity Four]. Reflect on this frustration looking back now as an adult, painting a picture of the moment and exploring differences between then and now.

Guiding Questions:
How has your perspective about such frustrations changed with time?
What was the result of such frustrations as a child?

Cats

Murakami cats, Kafka—the talk of cats.
Batting big bundles of words to the brim,
a beckoning cat breaking thoughts.
Could cats scratch words from ink?
Weird words work windowless wondering
into view,
deep cuts contouring cold copy—
lava into letters.

Cats

Bradbury cats, metaphors behind wry
smiles.
Fuzz, friction, fake inanimate intimacy
because fun favored fiction.
Could cats be Atwood's wolves,
howling under the moon—
masks more mutually mistaken as
curiosity in a pack, a place, a penance.

Cats

Tickled by city horns and motorbike purrs,
wild felines whisked into the homes of
worried widows.
Independence—an inside job.
Could we have been tricked?
Play the part, pet the pussy.
Here hails a human, hushed by hope that
we would be anything other than

Cats

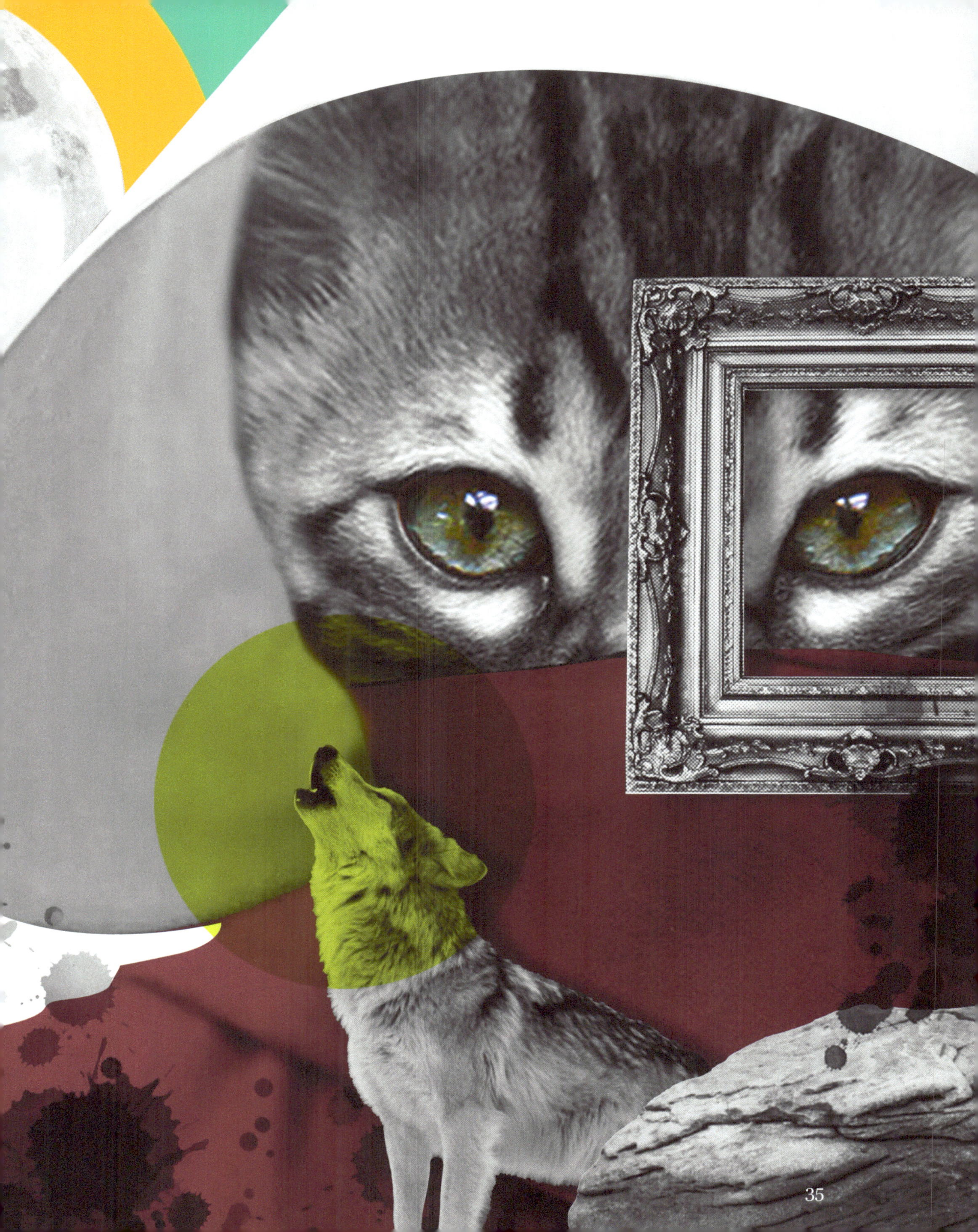

The Muse

At an engagement party in Casablanca, I met a fellow named Chad. He sat, shoulders squared, hands folded, confident on the couch next to his wife, Krista. Chad's beaming smile and youthful attention to anyone's story betrayed his tough exterior. Writing flowered in our conversation, Chad being a fan, having started quite a few short stories. However, he took a firm stance on his abilities only shining under one condition—depression. He hadn't written in years because he wasn't in "that place" anymore.

Elated to hear Chad had surpassed depression, my heart ached as he believed his art came at the cost of his happiness. His statement lingered because I was finding my own way through depression at the time—navigating the complexities of sobriety and grief. I wondered if on the other side of my depression, I'd lose the gusto in my work. The raw power brewing from pain.

Instead, I found what most strong writers find at one time or another—when you make space for creativity, she will find you, regardless of the emotional state you bring to the page. Pain is far from the *only* ingredient for great writing.

Each writer is seeking channels for creativity, some secret hand-me-down recipe to get the work done, and the recipe varies from writer to writer. Stephen King cites creativity coming from a rigorous schedule, a dedicated space where if the muse knows where you'll be, "sooner or later he'll start showing up, chomping his cigar and making his magic."[29]

In today's exercise, let's use fiction to generate secret recipes for stirring imagination.

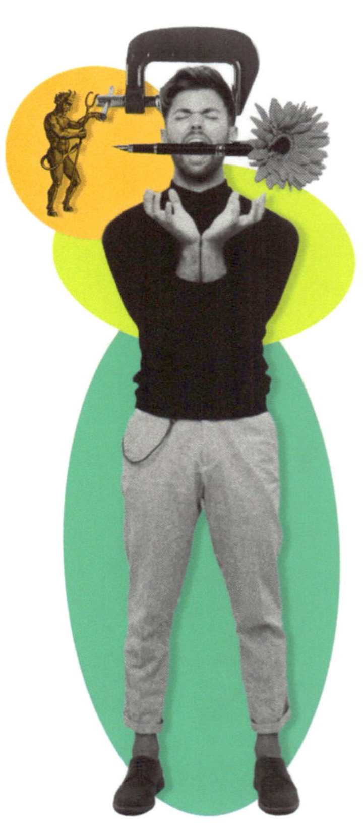

Your Writing Ritual:

► Stand or place your feet flat on the floor.
► Extend your arms out to the side.
► Draw in a breath while raising your arms above your head.
► Exhale while lowering your arms in front of your body.
► Repeat your breathing four times.
► Come back to center and shake out your hands.

Your Warm-Up:
Set your timer for 2 mins.
Answer the following question.
Trading places with a writer for a day, what would you hope to absorb about their process?

Activity One:
Set your timer for 2 mins.
Make a list of people or items you would trust to give advice about imagination. Examples: J. R. R. Tolkien
/ magicians / God / Magic 8 Ball

Activity Two:
Choose a person or an item from [Activity One].

Activity Three:
Set your timer for 2 mins.
Jot down notes on what writing advice you've heard around getting into the flow state. Examples: breathe
/ buckle yourself to the chair / proper stiff drink / just keep typing

Activity Four:
Set your timer for 2 mins.
Make a list of ingredients you would need if writing a recipe for stirring the imagination. Examples: potion
/ time / magic words / muse

Endurance Writing Prompt:
Set your timer for 15 mins.
You have the most sacred and sought-after recipe in history—a recipe for stirring the imagination.
Across the creative community, your recipe is in high demand. Write a narrative, blog style, to
introduce who you are [Activity Two] and spill the beans on the creative world's biggest secret.
Include ingredients for your recipe [Activity Three and Four] and step-by-step instructions for
success. Conclude your article with notes on who this recipe is ideally for and any cautionary notes
for the reader.

Guiding Questions:
What is the best case outcome if someone follows your recipe?
How did your trustworthy recipe maker come to discover the magic ingredients?

Collecting Dust

My mother keeps a plastic bin in the basement permanently tasked with collecting the items deemed junk for donation. I picked through its contents the last time I was home to see what hadn't made the cut. Beneath layers of sweaters and mismatched Tupperware, there was a statue of a bald eagle. The statue lived on the top of the glass bookcase at the end of the hall for more than thirty years. An ever-watchful guardian, collecting dust on duty. Every Easter, surely, the eagle held a Nestle chocolate egg to be discovered. The statue had no real significance for me, but I was saddened by its destiny. The eagle had been affixed to the landscape of the house. The hallway had less authority, more white space, when I noticed the statue was gone. I sat down to journal about all the memories of the eagle before it was fated to find another home on the shelves of our local second-hand ARC. I was surprised by all the ways this forgotten object unearthed scenes from my childhood home.

Objects, when pulled into our writing, can operate beyond filling white space. Objects tell stories, carry memories—they give definition, meaning to the world. In writing, an object has the ability to transport our perception or hold us captive to a moment. Objects have a way of anchoring themselves in a story; they can direct the entirety of plot. What would *Lord of The Rings: The Fellowship of The Ring* be without a ring? Or *The Picture of Dorian Gray* without his painting?

As writers, we can tune into the objects around us for inspiration. We can notice objects harbored past their obvious use or recall those tossed away without a second thought.

In today's exercise, let's explore how forgotten objects can drive a story.

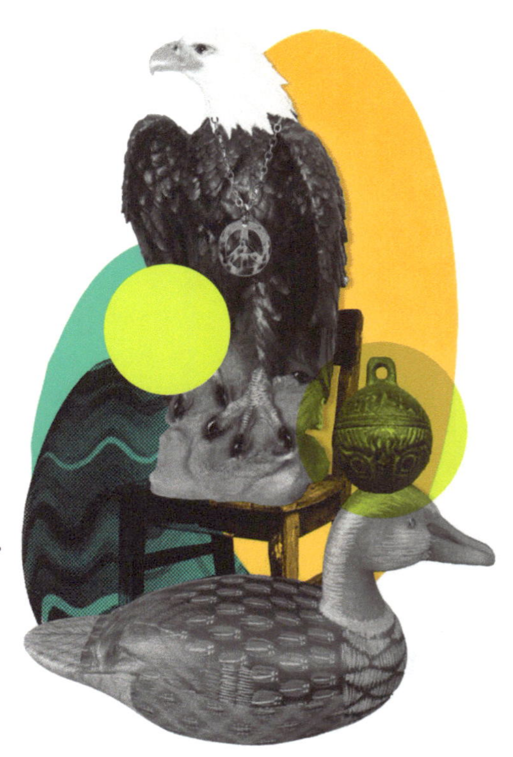

Set Your Intention For Today's Writing Practice

Your Writing Ritual:
▶ Stand tall with your feet firmly grounded.
▶ Bend your knees slightly and sway your hips side to side.
▶ Inhale as you sway left, exhale as you sway right.
▶ Keep your movement smooth and slow.
▶ Continue this rhythm for eight breaths.
▶ Come to stillness.

Your Warm-Up:
Set your timer for 2 mins.
Answer the following question.
What was the last thing you donated?

Activity One:
Set your timer for 2 mins.
Make a list of things you would put into a donation box. Examples: records / picture frame / ex-girlfriend's college hoodie / egg timer

Activity Two:
Set your timer for 2 mins.
Make a list of all the things a family member or partner might put into a donation box and not tell you about. Examples: baby blanket / Christmas mug with a family photo / the sweater you bought them for their birthday / your baby teeth

Activity Three:
Choose an item from either [Activity One] or [Activity Two].

Activity Four:
Set your timer for 2 mins.
Make a list of reasons why the item from [Activity Three] is being donated. Example: out with the old / moving sale / resentment / haunted by the object

Activity Five:
Choose a reason for donation from [Activity Four].

Activity Six:
Set your timer for 1 min.
Begin to think about a character and jot down details of who would be most affected by the item donated.

Endurance Writing Prompt:
Set your timer for 15 mins.
A character [Activity Six] goes to the second-hand shop when they notice something unique on the shelf. On further inspection, they're convinced [Activity Three] was once theirs. Jump into a scene where your character rediscovers memories of this item and ponders the reasons for its donation [Activity Five]. Show us what happens next.

Guiding Questions:
What would it look like for your character to confront the person who donated the item?
Why do they even care that the item is up for sale to total strangers in a thrift shop?

Freedom

One of the greatest examples of oratory work in the 21st century is Martin Luther King Jr.'s "I Have A Dream" speech. The young preacher's words spill like syrup across the page—sticky, sweet, thick with meaning. He stirs our hearts with his apt metaphors of hills, promissory notes, songs, and dreams to build a vision of change. His persuasive techniques are deeply tied to poetic symbolism. Annually, I listen to his speech given from the steps of the Lincoln Memorial. Last year, I wanted to explore freedom and oppression in my writing workshop, mirroring Martin Luther King Jr.'s metaphoric flair.

The concept of freedom, however, loomed as both taboo and somewhat untouchable, being that I hosted the workshop in a culture not my own. As a heterosexual, able-bodied, white woman with an American passport, how could I wrap my arms around the grand concept of freedom at a table in Morocco? A table of writers with varying backgrounds, beliefs, sexual orientations, preferences, and privileges?

We did so through art.

Writing for many centuries has been a way to discover one's self. To broach taboos around freedom and oppression, the expectation was reflection. To let art be the medium. Let symbols bear the burden. Let metaphor be the hook to hold our reflections and first-hand experiences. I want to romanticize the moment. What happened instead was honesty—at times discomfort. Truth upon truth, each writer filled their page. Compelled to use their voice even if only inside their journals.

In today's exercise, let's dig into your voice and create a picture of freedom painted from your lived experiences.

Definitions:
▸ Oppression: unjust or cruel exercise of authority or power
  Freedom: the power or right to act, speak, or think as one wants.
  The state of not being imprisoned or enslaved.

Set Your Intention For Today's Writing Practice

Your Writing Ritual:
▸ Sit or stand with your spine aligned.
▸ Inhale through your nose and lift your shoulders to your ears.
▸ Exhale forcefully through your mouth and drop your shoulders.
▸ Repeat five times.
▸ Roll your neck gently from side to side.
▸ Shake out your hands.

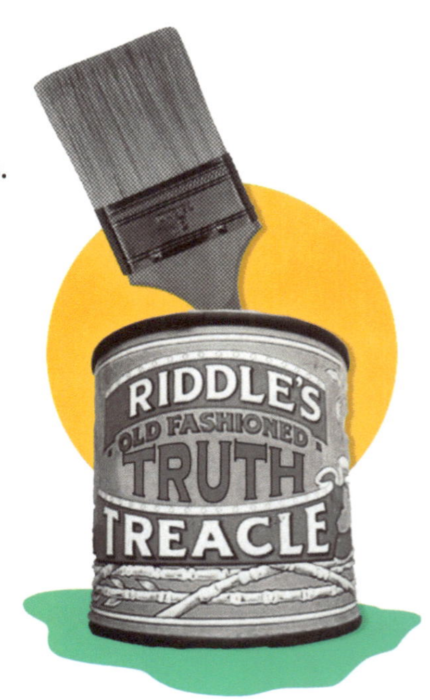

Your Warm-Up:
Set your timer for 2 mins.
Answer the following question.
What does it feel like in your body when you hear the word freedom?

Activity One:
Set your timer for 2 mins.
Make a list of symbols you might associate with the word freedom. Examples: birds / bells / flags / fire

Activity Two:
Set your timer for 2 mins.
Make a list of symbols you might associate with oppression. Examples: shackles / smoke / rope / duct tape

Activity Three:
Set your timer for 2 mins.
List examples of oppression. Think about areas of society where oppression might linger and how it persists (education, politics, media). Examples: denied access to education / bound by borders / pay gap / shaming sex before marriage

Activity Four:
Set your timer for 2 mins.
List as many examples of what freedom looks like in your personal life. Examples: the freedom of religion /access to travel / love marriage / access to spaces based on the color of my skin

Endurance Writing Prompt:
Set your timer for 15 mins.
Use first-person experience to answer two key questions: what is oppression and what is freedom? Draw from all of your creative examples above. Stretch yourself to tie symbols from [Activity One] and [Activity Two] with examples from [Activity Three] and [Activity Four].

Guiding Questions:
What feelings arise as you use examples and symbols?
What would someone expect to see painted on a wall with a theme of freedom?

An Adult Picture Book

Author Adam Mansbach changed the landscape of picture books when he published *Go The Fuck to Sleep*. The book's popularity, in part, is because of Adam's abrupt honesty around parenting—the gig is tough. However, his story captivated more than just parents—the book reached number one on Amazon. Mansbach and his creative partner Ricardo Cortés launched as a small Facebook project, but their popularity worldwide inspired more in the genre of adult picture books like *All My Friends Are Dead*, *Nobody Likes A Cockblock*, and *K Is For Knifeball: A Book Of Terrible Advice*.

Like Vladimir Nabokov did with *Lolita* in fiction or Elvis did with rock and roll, charging against the status quo is how artists create art. The use of expletives, satire, and lack of empathy flips what we know about the beloved format of a children's book. Mansbach lined the flesh of the genre with the circulatory system of adult issues, authoring simple though not easy concepts. As writers, we hope to write with honesty, thwarting taboo in our art. As seen in the adult picture book genre, by wielding satire, our heavy thoughts land lightly for our readers.

In today's exercise, let's use the structure of a children's book to write about adult themes.

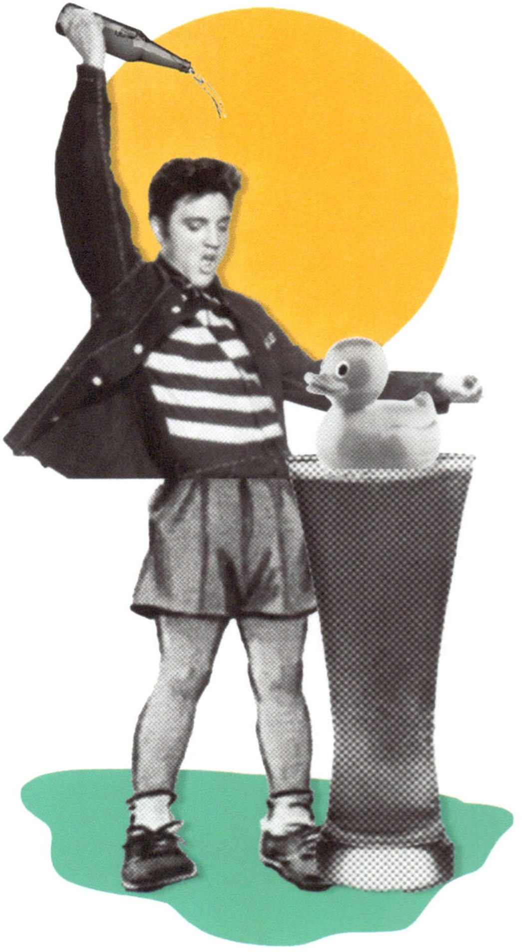

Set Your Intention For Today's Writing Practice

Your Writing Ritual:
- Stand or sit with a long spine.
- Gently tap your fingertips on your collarbones.
- Inhale through your nose and hum as you exhale.
- Repeat the breath and hum four times.
- Drop your hands and shake them out.
- Roll your shoulders back three times.

Set your timer for 2 mins.
Answer the following question.
What life lessons or morals do you recall learning from children's books?

Activity One:
Set your timer for 2 mins.
Make a list of themes you wish you could read about as an adult, in a picture book format. Examples: dating / capitalism / mental health / making a roux

Activity Two:
Choose a theme from [Activity One].

Activity Three:
Set your timer for 2 mins.
Based on the theme from [Activity Two], brainstorm on possible events happening around this theme. Examples for dating: first time dating after a divorce leads to speed-dating / hook-up apps / pole dancing classes for confidence / championing a new solo journey

Activity Four:
Set your timer for 2 mins
Make a list of possible moral conclusions an adult might come to around your theme from [Activity One]. Examples for dating: Love yourself so you can then love others. / It's a numbers game. / The law of attraction is no joke. / Love will find you where you're at.

Activity Five:
Set your timer for 1 min.
Decide on a mythical protagonist through whom a story can be told. Examples: pirate / a happy aura / a sponge / unicorn

Endurance Writing Prompt:
Set your timer for 15 mins.
You're authoring a new adult picture book about [Activity Two]. Your character [Activity Five] moves through a timeline of events [Activity Three]. Keep your plot moving with simple, direct actions. Carry us toward a final moral(s) [Activity Four].

Guiding Questions:
How does your protagonist act in each situation?
How can you increase the intensity of events to grow your protagonist?

A Thimble Of Firsts

One of my favorite feelings is the sensation of reading a fantastic book for the first time.
The energy of good writing electrifies my fingers to turn the pages, the thoughts provoked and
nurtured by a story well written. I am the type to turn the last page of a book, close the binding,
and hold the book to my chest. I can still feel the searing beauty of Ocean Vuong's *On Earth We're
Briefly Gorgeous*, the tremendous empathy for *The Faraway Nearby,* the heartbreak in closing
the pages of *Cloud Cuckoo Land.* The feeling of joy or sadness or enlightenment is so great that I
am consumed by a want to hold its energy forever. I'm a romantic, a sentimentalist, and I hold
first experiences in serious regard.

As an adult, it's more comfortable to get lost in routine and miss the excitement, terror, treasure
of experiencing something for the very first time. It's easy to flutter through the motion of time to
get caught in life's thick mud of mundane. As conscious beings, we can choose how to review our
first kiss, our first time away from home, the first time we ate shrimp, or dove into a body of
water. Firsts can have all the meaning in the world or no meaning at all. As a writer, however,
a series of firsts, great and small, can animate your stories. With more focus, you can write as an
explorer in the newness of every moment. In writing, you can observe, muse, reveal, awe, and
wonder about your lived experience.

In today's exercise, let's explore a series of first experiences
in your life and how they make up your story.

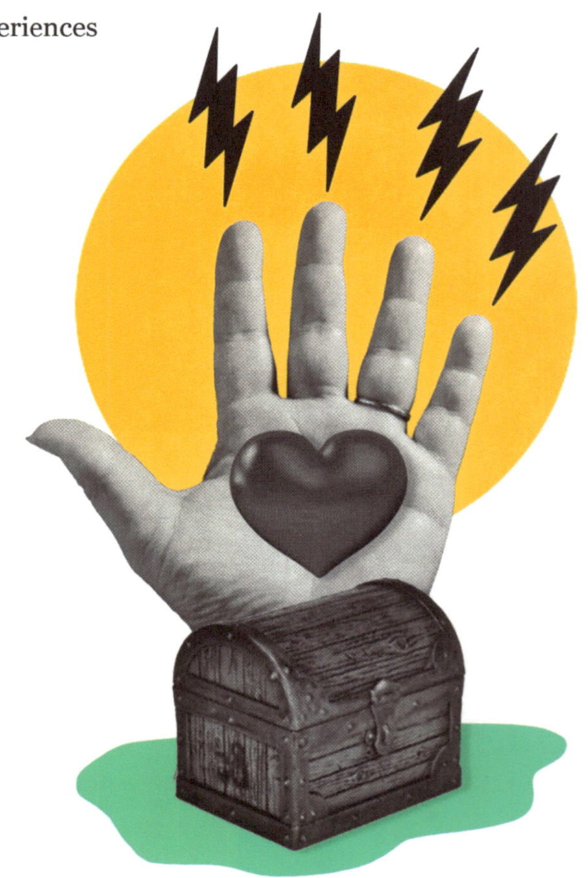

Set Your Intention For Today's Writing Practice

Your Writing Ritual:

- ▶ Sit with your spine tall and feet flat.
- ▶ Close your eyes and gently press your palms
  together at your heart.
- ▶ Inhale through your nose to the count of four.
- ▶ Exhale through your mouth to the count of five.
- ▶ Repeat this breathing pattern six times.
- ▶ Drop your hands and roll your shoulders.

Set your timer for 2 mins.

Answer the following question.

What was it like the first time you were seriously injured as a kid?

Activity One:
Set your timer for 2 mins.

Make a list of "firsts," events, moments, or milestones that one might experience in their life.

Examples: had sex / failed miserably / moved out / touched snow

Activity Two:
Set your timer for 2 mins.

Make a list of personal "firsts," events, moments, or milestones that complete the sentence "It was the first time I…" Examples: said a swear word / got robbed / had a beer / read my published work

Activity Three:
Set your timer for 2 mins.

Make a list of questions you might ask someone to answer to elaborate on their first experience of an event, moment, or milestone. Examples: What smell was in the air? / Who else noticed? / Where would you have liked to have been when this happened? / Why was this first significant?

Activity Four:
Choose a first from either [Activity One] or [Activity Two].

Activity Five:
Choose a question from [Activity Three].

Endurance Writing Prompt:
Set your timer for 15 mins.

Write a nonfiction narrative about the first time you [Activity Four]. Paint us a picture of your experience. Use your senses and inner thoughts to re-create the memory or offer us a reflection of the memory. Let [Activity Five] be your launching question as you pull us into the memory.

Guiding Questions:
What were the leading events (rising action) to this first experience, and what followed (falling action)? How was this first, either something to check off the list or something you would have avoided if possible?

Salmon Is The Color Of Flesh

Science, in broad strokes, is the field of study in understanding the world. Writing, too, in all its encompassing breadth, is a field of study about the world. Where science and writing blossom from a similar seed is in their innate nature of curiosity. The two fields have varying approaches to answering big life questions, but both wield their craft as a means to give us a broader perspective. To challenge us to explore truth, debunk myth, or explain the unexplainable. Both require a relentless optimism to run the experiments over again until, exhausting all angles, they arrive at a solitary conclusion, even if that conclusion is inconclusive.

As the poet C. Day Lewis wrote, "I do not sit down at my desk to put into verse something that is already clear in my mind... We do not write in order to be understood; we write in order to understand."[33]

Writing, similar to science, is a labor of comprehension. As writers, we test hypotheses, tweaking perspective, connection, truth, desire, or reality to see the patterned effects of human nature, of existence. What if, to build your writing muscles, we borrowed the synthesized scientific style of reporting as a vehicle of play and curiosity in our writing? Where in creative writing we have the capability of being verbose, in science, being direct in observation without grandeur is key.

In today's exercise, let's explore curiosity about the world through scientific reporting.

Set Your Intention For Today's Writing Practice

Your Writing Ritual:

- Stand tall with your feet grounded.
- Bend slightly at the knees and bounce gently.
- Inhale deeply through your nose.
- Exhale with sound through your mouth.
- Continue bouncing and breathing for ten seconds.
- Stop and take one final grounding breath.

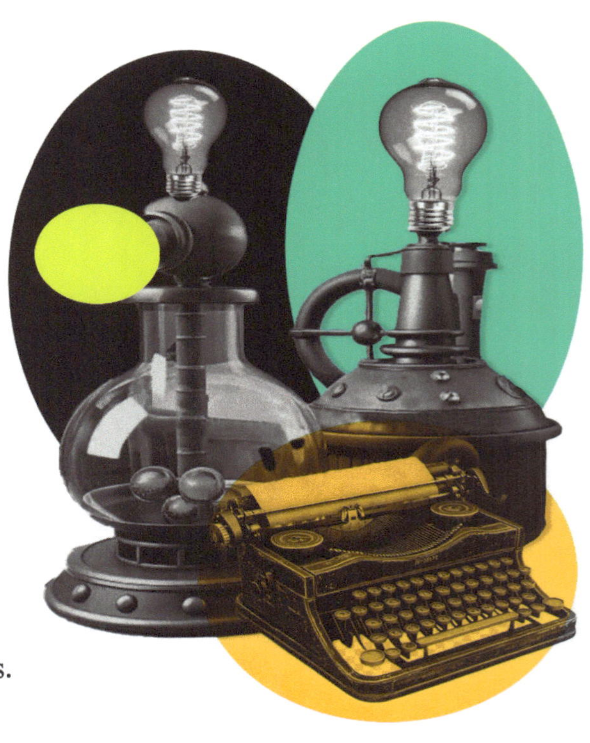

Your Warm-Up:

Set your timer for 2 mins.

Answer the following question.

How do you go about solving curiosities in your personal life?

Activity One:

Set your timer for 1 min.

Make a list of things a scientist might conduct experiments about. Examples: measuring the plastic particles in drinking water / measuring how much methane a cow releases into the atmosphere / measuring the spread of a virus / seeking a cure to lactose intolerance

Activity Two:

Set your timer for 1 min.

Make a list of all the things a scientist would not likely attempt to measure or experiment with. Examples: emotional connectedness to bees / checked vs. unchecked ratio of a dictator's to-do list / tracking farts between meals / the effect of the word "moist" on their test subject

Activity Three:

Set your timer for 2 mins.

Make a list of theoretical questions that a scientist might try to test to understand aspects of their personal life. Examples: What color shirt is most likely to seal the deal for a sexual encounter on a first date? / What is the effect on my ego of being called an asshole vs. a nerd? / How does one "lose" one's mind? / Can eating a single M&M vs. two at a time lead to greater intelligence?

Activity Four:

Choose one question from [Activity Three].

Activity Five:

Set your timer for 2 mins.

Generate a single fictional hypothesis considering the scientific question you chose in [Activity Four]. You can use an *if this* → *then what* → because structure to create your hypothesis. Example: If I wear a salmon colored shirt, then I will engage in sexual intercourse following a first date because salmon is the color of flesh. / If called an asshole by a stranger, my ego deflates because of my survival instincts to blend in with the pack.

Endurance Writing Prompt:

Set your timer for 15 mins.

Imagine you're a scientist trying to unpack the mysteries of life outside the lab. You're curious to discover more about [Activity Four] your personal life. Because you work best when thinking in terms of science, you've decided to conduct an experiment to prove or disprove the hypothesis of [Activity Five]. Use simple language and a technical step-by-step writing style to draw up the fictional report of your personal experiment.

Guiding Questions:

Where are you starting from, or what is your constant (unchanging) in the experiment?

Where do things blow up and distort your experiment?

The Write Space

When I write at a coffee shop, I search for the longest wooden table in the room. I need a tall chair to swing my legs, getting out my writing jitters. I need a maximum amount of surface to land the grand ideas brewing. My home office is the same. An eight-foot table full of writing books, sticky notes, pens, but always cleared with a few feet of open space for imagination to cartwheel. Knowing the ingredients of a comfortable writing space makes the stirring of creative work a savory stew. I'm less inclined to fidget or waste time tweaking something in my environment to be just right because I know, through continually showing up, that a big table is all I need.

Stephen King says that all you need is a desk and a white wall. Your bright red bucket of experience is the paint needed to splatter the textured white wall of your writing space. To write, we have to find the white wall or the big table through trial and error. Perhaps you require the hustle of life in a coffee shop, as many authors did in Paris in the '20s. You might need total isolation, like Emily Dickinson or Harper Lee. You may need the flexibility of writing wherever there's room, say the kitchen table as Haruki Murakami did when writing his first three novels. You have to develop a deep appreciation for creative space, one fitting for you, so you can get to the work of writing.

In today's exercise, let's explore your current writing space through a catalog of observations.

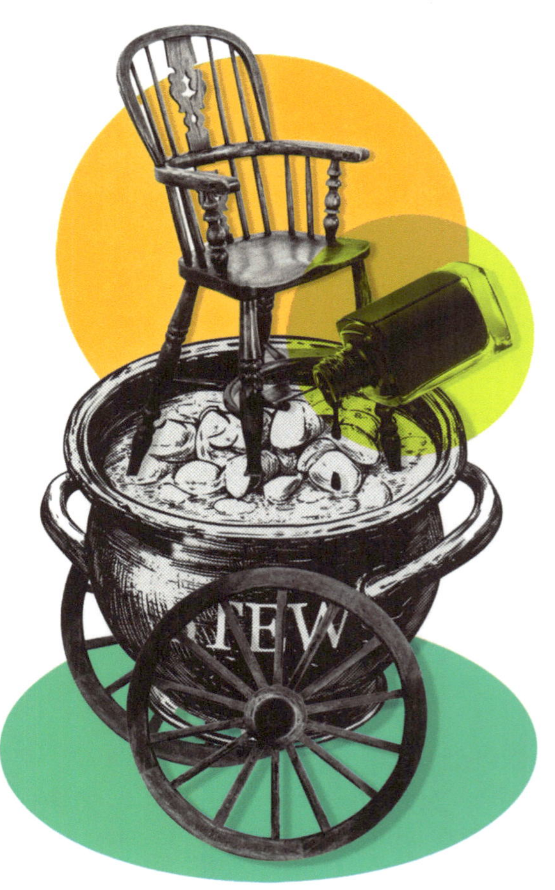

Set Your Intention For Today's Writing Practice

Your Writing Ritual:
- Sit with your spine straight and your feet grounded.
- Place your hands over your ribs.
- Inhale and feel your ribs expand.
- Exhale and feel them contract.
- Continue for five deep breaths.
- Release your hands and circle your wrists.

Set your timer for 2 mins.
Answer the following question.
What's the best writing space you've ever encountered?

Activity One:
Set your timer for 3 mins.
Make a list of all the elements of a perfect writing space for you. Examples: long wooden table / unlimited coffee / rain sounds / no clocks

Activity Two:
Set your timer for 1 min.
Make a list of items you can see in the space where you're sitting now. Examples: a stack of writing books / six bamboo scent sticks / two leather bar stools / muddy running shoes

Activity Three:
Set your timer for 1 min.
Make a list of sounds (or the absence of sound) you can hear in the space where you're sitting now. Examples: the tumble of concrete mixing on the street / birds whistling / the wheeze of my dog's breath while he sleeps / the trumpet, piano, and bass dancing through the speaker

Activity Four:
Set your timer for 1 min.
Jot down a series of observations about how this space makes you feel when you think about writing. Examples: expansive / anxious with the rhythm of the music / distracted / protected

Endurance Writing Prompt:
Set your timer for 15 mins.
Describe your ideal writing space. Use aspects of your dreamy writing corner from [Activity One] to create the scene. Allow the environment to engulf us as the reader through your details [Activity Three]. Help us feel your energy [Activity Four] by laying it all out on the page.

Guiding Questions:
How can you jump into this from a place of feeling and build outward?
What happens if you incorporate countable nouns (two books) in your description as you build?

Bedbugs

I spent two and a half years teaching English as a second language online for children primarily in China. For twenty-minute lessons, I tempered the pace of my speaking voice and utilized my expressive hand gestures to iterate English grammar. One of the concepts I enjoyed teaching was compound words.

Seven-year-olds mirrored my two balled fists, each representing a separate noun, bashing together to make a new compound word. There lay a sense of joy in how two things came together to create a new idea. At least, that's how I saw it. Who knows, maybe students just enjoyed bumping their fists together. I relished observing my students smash fists repeatedly chanting words like jellyfish, airport, cowboy, and fingerprint. I shared this joy in a conversation with my mother.

She mulled over the idea of compound words and then asked, "What if bedbugs were bugs who carried our beds?"

The jarring tangent to our conversation is much to my mother's character. She is always channeling new perspectives when I bring her thoughts on language and writing. She is one of the earliest inspirations I have of letting curiosity guide your creativity.

We dashed into a conversation around compound words, skinned and reshaped to new definitions. We stuck on bedbugs for a minute. We mused about a needle-sized-red-butt beetle of bedding we all despise to instead, be a humble insect of service to the big city, hauling the weight of California-King-sized beds across Manhattan. The image gave me chills, the kind I get when I know I've landed on a fun new idea.

With a pinch of play, compound words have an infinite landscape of redirecting your images. A keyboard becomes a group of board members made of cold golden keys. A sunflower becomes the dry ingredient in the kitchen to make cosmic cookies. The beauty of language is how it's wielded by the speaker. To write is to imagine and to re-imagine.

In today's exercise, let's explore compound words to re-imagine their meaning.

Definition:

▸ Compound words: when two or more words or signs are joined to make a longer word or sign that differs from those of the words they're made of.

Set Your Intention For Today's Writing Practice

Your Writing Ritual:

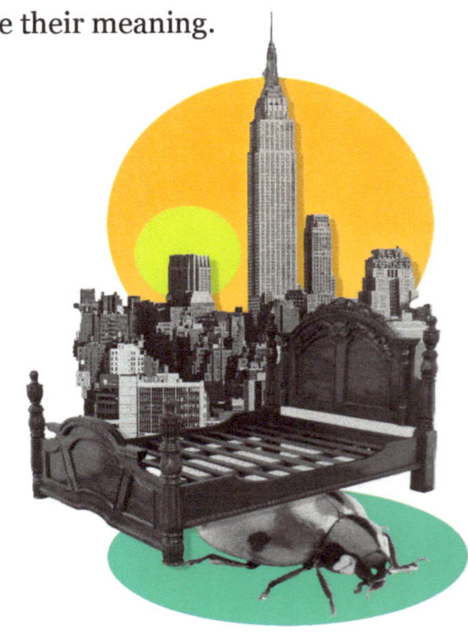

▸ Sit tall and bring your palms together in front of your chest.
▸ Inhale through your nose.
▸ As you exhale, gently press your palms together.
▸ Inhale and release the pressure.
▸ Repeat this breath and press cycle six times.
▸ Drop your hands and wiggle your fingers.

Your Warm-Up:
Set your timer for 2 mins.
Answer the following question.
What was your experience like learning English grammar growing up?

Activity One:
Set your timer for 2 mins.
Create a list of compound words.
Examples: rainbow / jellyfish / cowboy / breadbox

Activity Two:
Set your timer for 1 min.
For each of the compound words above, reverse the order of the words and create a new image of the two words. Examples: a bow made of rain / fish made of strawberry jelly / boots worn by a cow / a box constructed of sourdough bread

Activity Three:
Pick one of the reverse compound words from [Activity Two].

Activity Four:
Using the reverse compound word from [Activity Three], pull together pieces of a story beginning with the who, what, when, where, and why for this idea. Example: a bow made of rain: Zeus had a bow made of rain when one Sunday from high on Mt. Olympus his bow dried up.

Endurance Writing Promt:
Set your timer for 15 mins.
Start to build a story inspired from the reverse compound word picked in [Activity Three].
Let your imagination roam. Build the foundation around this idea using the interrogative questions in [Activity Four]. Let the idea flow to see where a story forms. Let creativity take over.

Guiding Questions:
Who is surprised by this reversal of the order of things, this new reality?
What is turned upside down in the reversal of these compound words?

Reading: The Gateway Drug To Writing

A classic case of "right place, right time" landed Katrina in my creative writing workshop in March of last year. She had minimal expectations, but to attend because her son, Daniel, was a regular at my workshop. She leaned in, writing flash fiction in our 15 minutes of endurance writing. Her writing poured over the page with the ease of reciting a familiar bedtime story. She had a clean grasp of story arcs, of conflict. Her characters took on the page with presence. Katrina wrote with honesty, with confidence, that I imagined she'd practiced for many years. I learned Katrina had no formal background in writing. She did, however, have more than 1,000 books in her home library. Novels she consumes daily. She's spent her life reading, devoted to a love of reading, as her son told me. With a deep devotion to reading, writing came to her with ease.

As a writer, your love for storytelling is fed by an equal love of reading. To read is to explore. To read is to enable your curiosity. To read is to develop your understanding of the human experience. As Stephen King writes, "If you want to be a writer, you must do two things above all others: read a lot and write a lot."[28] If you have an interest in writing, you must have an equal interest in reading. Whether you consume John Grisham's latest bestseller, Toni Morrison's profound fiction, or David Sedaris's acute satire, reading enables you to pull on the suit of a writer. Like Gregory David Roberts writes in *Shantaram*, "everything in life has an effect on you greater than zero."[50] One step further, everything you read has an effect on your writing greater than zero.

In today's exercise, let's write letters about the effect reading has on your love for writing.

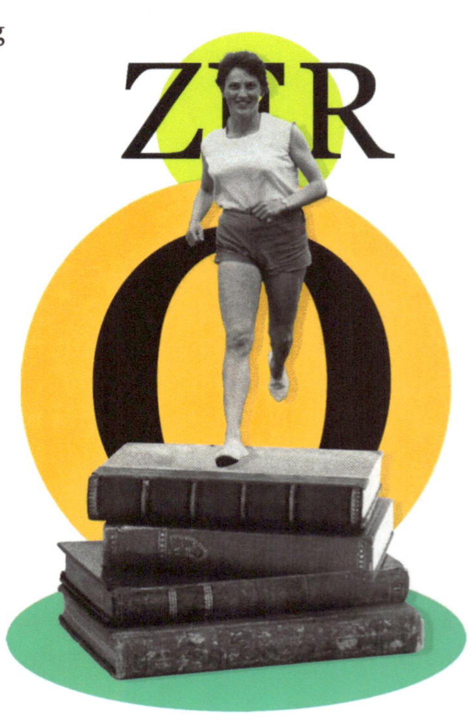

Set Your Intention For Today's Writing Practice

Your Writing Ritual:

▸ Sit or stand with your feet flat on the ground.
▸ Inhale and draw your shoulders up to your ears.
▸ Hold your breath for a count of three.
▸ Exhale with a sigh and drop your shoulders completely.
▸ Repeat this shoulder lift and release five times.
▸ Shake out your shoulders and arms to loosen any tension.

Set your timer for 2 mins.
Answer the following question.
What is the first chapter book you remember reading as a kid?

Activity One:
Set your timer for 2 mins.
Make a list of books you read as a kid. Examples: *The Berenstain Bears* / *Arthur* / *A Series of Unfortunate Events* / *The Giver*

Activity Two:
Set your timer for 2 mins.
Make a list of all the ways reading has a positive effect on an individual. Examples: teaches empathy / stirs imagination / enables great storytelling / provides truth

Activity Three:
Set your timer for 3 mins.
Jot down thoughts on the first book you remember binge reading, providing the who, what, when, and where.

Endurance Writing Prompt:
Set your timer for 15 mins.
Write a letter to your younger self, hoping to convey how much reading will unlock worlds of possibilities for your future. Highlight the books most impactful in your early life [Activity One]. Acknowledge the first time you remember binge reading a book [Activity Three]. Zoom in on the ways reading has helped you grow over the years [Activity Two].

Guiding Questions:
How would your life be different if you were illiterate?
When did you realize reading was something you enjoyed?

The Shape-Shifting Tiger

When my writing practice is fluid, my dreams are vivid. I love spending the first twenty minutes of my writing day recalling the night's dreams. I sit with my eyes closed at the computer and type. The rhythm of my writing for each dream is sharp, punchy, incoherent.

One night I'll befriend a bear on ecstasy, another I'm captain of a cloud ship. I write what I can remember. I cut from scene to scene when there is a gap. I write without editing, without exaggeration.

In his book on writing, *Zen In The Art Of Writing*, Ray Bradbury hints at this wealth of imagination we all carry. "When people ask me where I get my ideas, I laugh. How strange—we're so busy looking out, to find ways and means, we forget to look in."[5]

Dream writing is a way to look inward. A way to connect with ideas in more free-form. It's tempting in a first draft to indulge the delete button, to hold a blade against bubbling ideas. Dream writing allows the shape-shifting tiger of imagination—too cunning, too quick—to outrun the hungry nature of the backspace bar on your keyboard. Dreams are messy, loud, tyrants of logic bent on existence rather than reason. Therefore, when given free rein of a blank page and a medium of dictation where you allow yourself to step out of the way, the result is salacious. When you can allow yourself to record your dreams, you are flexing your creative muscles.

In today's exercise, let's create a smattering of dreamlike images.

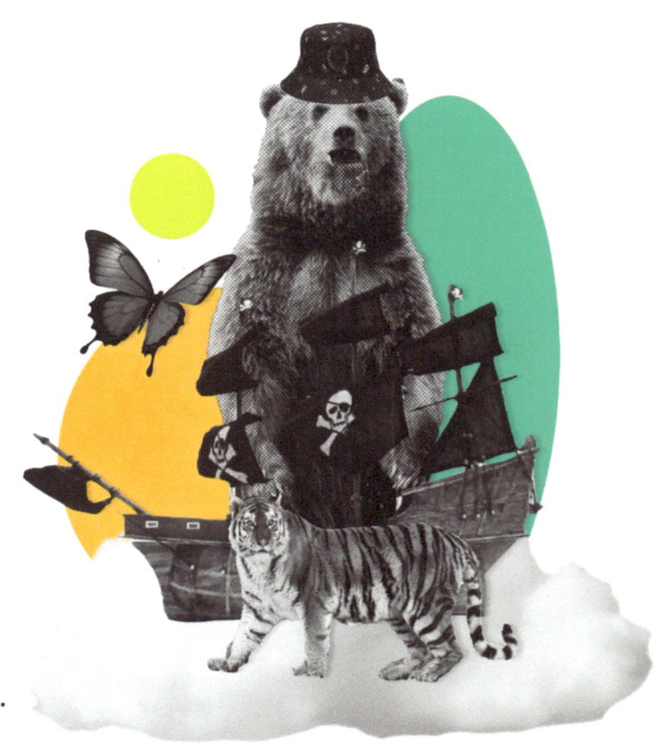

Set Your Intention For Today's Writing Practice

Your Writing Ritual:

- ▸ Sit with your hands on your belly.
- ▸ Inhale slowly through your nose.
- ▸ Exhale with a soft "ssss" sound.
- ▸ Repeat the breath and sound five times.
- ▸ Rub your hands together to create warmth.
- ▸ Place them gently over your heart.

Your Warm-Up:

Set your timer for 2 mins.
Answer the following question.
How do your dreams play a role in your life?

Activity One:

Set your timer for 2 mins.
Make a list of the fantastical elements from any book or movie with a dream element—think *Through The Looking Glass, Inception.* Examples: talking cats / shapeshifting buildings / hookah smoking caterpillar / objects growing or shrinking

Activity Two:

Set your timer for 2 mins.
Use bullet points to outline the sequence of events from your life the day before. Examples: snoozed the alarm / yoga / short story writing / laundry

Activity Three:

Set your timer for 2 mins.
For each of the bullet points in the list from [Activity One], animate the event by imagining a fantastical twist. Examples: snoozed the alarm: My hand became an analog clock. / yoga: I folded into a salted caramel pretzel. / short story writing: The computer burped letters on the desk. / laundry: The world spun while the washing stood still.

Endurance Writing Prompt:
Set your timer for 15 mins.
Create a lucid dream sequence by connecting real events from [Activity Two] with fantastical elements from [Activity Three]. Think about using all of your senses to liven the images. Mirror the sporadic movement of a dream by challenging yourself to write without conjunctions (and / or / but / so).

Guiding Questions:
What were you driven to accomplish in the dream that kept getting interrupted?
When did you realize something wasn't right in the dream?

In Pen We Appreciate

A trunk full of collected birthday cards and notes from my childhood waits in storage. Notes from my mother, kindergarten friends, relatives passed, friends present, all settled in the dust of waiting to be read again. Most cards I keep, held because of the handwriting, not the words, but there is one card I carry with me and post up in my office where I write. On thick cream-colored cardstock paper folded over is a card with my name on the front. Left in my dorm room from when I lived in Ireland for a semester. The handwriting inside the card is big. The letters with legs smoothly curled, a tease of cursive. The birthday wishes inside the folded card are lofty, imaginative, poetic, and the card is unsigned. A gift of words.

Frustrated by the anonymous card at first, the anonymity gave way to excitement. The words had movement and beauty. The words had life.

Oscar Wilde says, "Man is least himself when he talks in his own person. Give him a mask, and he'll tell you the truth."[65] Without an author, the message holds the spotlight, the words hold honesty.

Writing anonymously eliminates a preconceived identity for your words. Without claiming your writing in a card or a letter, a comment, or a message in a bottle, you lend your reader a more consumable truth. They have no choice but to take your words as they are, detached from identity and disconnected from external biases.

In today's exercise, let's explore writing anonymous letters of appreciation.

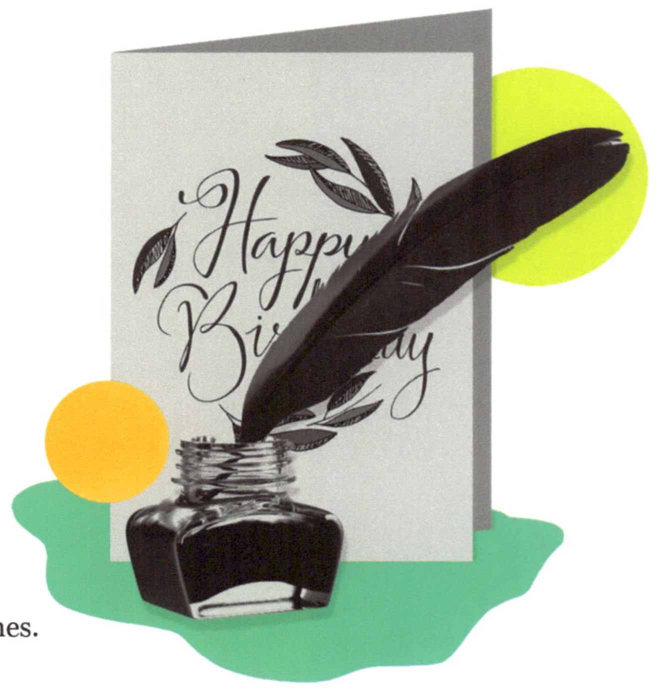

Set Your Intention For Today's Writing Practice

Your Writing Ritual:

- Stand with your feet flat on the floor.
- Interlace your fingers behind your back and press out in a stretch.
- Inhale deeply through your nose, opening your chest.
- Exhale through your mouth and soften your shoulders.
- Repeat this breath and stretch cycle five times.
- Release your hands and shake them out.

Set your timer for 2 mins.
Answer the following question.
Describe the last time you wrote a letter to someone?

Activity One:

Set your timer for 2 mins.
Make a list of all the people you may interact with on a daily basis. Examples: grocery store cashier
/ a postal worker / the woman from 2b / your boss

Activity Two:

Choose a person from [Activity One].

Activity Three:

Set your timer for 2 mins.
Jot down ideas of how this person has made a difference in your life or in your community. Examples
for a postal worker: a messenger of good news / a rock in the system of snail mail / an internal part of
shepherding bills / a connector of families far apart

Endurance Writing Prompt:

Set your timer for 15 mins.
Write an anonymous letter of appreciation to a person in your community [Activity Two]. You can
lean into all the ways you've been positively affected by their presence [Activity Three]. Move into
describing what you hope the letter might achieve.

Guiding Questions:

What would happen if they ceased to be part of the community in the way they are now?
What might you appreciate hearing in an anonymous letter of appreciation?

Jump On The Bandwagon

The instructional reference books *Dummies* emerged in the early '90s. The hard-to-master suddenly became the easy-to-learn. Everything from computer science to knitting became a viable pursuit. The titles motioned a sensational wave of reading to know through direct, tangible terms. The *Dummies* books lean into our continual lust for learning. A nod to our innate nature to figure out how the world works, a sixty-page book that validates your curiosity for decluttering, retiring racing greyhounds, or beekeeping. Each reference guide utilizes sharp, simple prose as the vehicle of transformation from dummy to distinguished.

In a broad application of writing, technical writing gets a bad rap for being creatively vapid against the spectacle of fiction. However, even within the parameters of imperative writing, we have an opportunity to polish our literary tools. The technical realm of manuals, terms and conditions pages, operational procedures, and how-to guides requires a recipe of concise clarity. Technical writing is the art of the precision of compounding steps, the command of a greater vision. As writers, we can use the framework of reference writing as an exercise in priming our writing muscles.

In today's exercise, let's play with technical writing to create how-to guides.

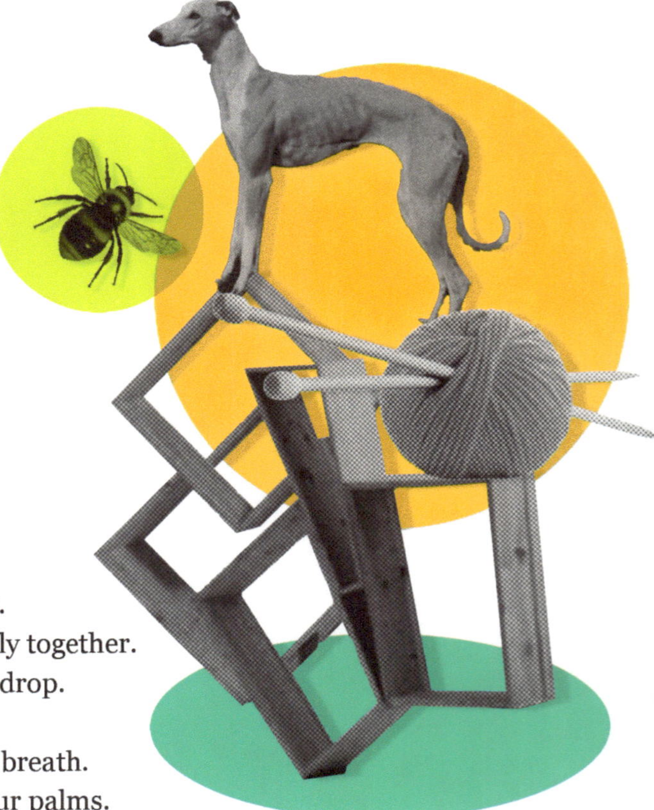

Set Your Intention For Today's Writing Practice

Your Writing Ritual:

- Sit with your hands lightly cupping your knees.
- Inhale while pulling your shoulder blades gently together.
- Exhale and curve your spine, letting your chin drop.
- Repeat this seated cat-cow motion four times.
- Return to upright posture and take one steady breath.
- Stretch your arms forward and slowly open your palms.

Your Warm-Up:

Set your timer for 2 mins.
Answer the following question.
If you had all the time and space in the world, what would you like to learn how to do?

Activity One:

Set your timer for 2 mins.
Make a list of things you are a die-hard fan of, where others might think your interests are quirky.
Examples: reading dystopian novels / bacon / mid-day dance parties / bird calls

Activity Two:

Pick something you're a die-hard fan of from [Activity One].

Activity Three:

Set your timer for 2 mins.
Jot down ideas on how you would recognize a fellow die-hard fan. Examples for bacon: a happy dance while eating bacon / ordering a side of bacon with their bacon / PBJ sandwich with bacon / a birthday cake flavored like bacon families far apart

Activity Four:

Set your timer for 2 mins.
Make a list of rookie mistakes someone might make when trying to jump on the bandwagon of fandom for [Activity Two]. Examples for bacon: not crisping their bacon / accepting turkey bacon as real bacon / sharing their bacon rations / not having a backup portion of bacon

Endurance Writing Prompt:

Set your timer for 15 mins.
Imagine you are the go-to expert for [Activity Two]. Dive in using plain language to create a step-by-step guide on how to jump on the bandwagon for your specific item of fandom. Pull in attributes from [Activity Three] and popular rookie mistakes from [Activity Four] to ensure that readers are transformed from newbie to know-it-all.

Guiding Questions:

How will the reader know when they've achieved the transformation of being a true fan?
What might a true fan wear?

Runny Eggs

Eggs do not have legs to run, nor cake batter a body to fold. A roast is without a bottom to rest, nor bread baring feet to rise. Yet, we marry action to so many aspects of cuisine. Roald Dahl does this best in his novel *Charlie and the Chocolate Factory*. Dahl's imaginative prose of candy-coated dreams makes a playground of mealtime, magnifying the magic in the things we eat through a literal lens of the verbal attributes. For "whipped cream isn't whipped cream at all if it hasn't been whipped with whips, just like poached eggs isn't poached eggs unless it's been stolen in the dead of the night."[7]

Suddenly, cream and eggs are an active sentence on the page. He animates our sense of wonder—rainbow drops—while plating food as both physical and creative nourishment: "suck them and you can spit in six different colours."[7] In his work, food takes on a world of magic and youthful excitement, transformed by a play on word association.

We see, through Dahl, how bland mealtime prose can be sautéed with richer word choice. As writers, we can pepper palatable verbs against edible items as a new way to approach a stale topic. Writing with food at the forefront of your images is a way to draw the reader in through alternate senses.

In today's exercise, let's write with active verbs to engage our reader by their tastebuds.

Definition:
▸ Verb: a word (such as jump, happen, or exist) that functions as the main word of the predicate of a sentence and expresses an act, occurrence, or state of being.

Set Your Intention For Today's Writing Practice

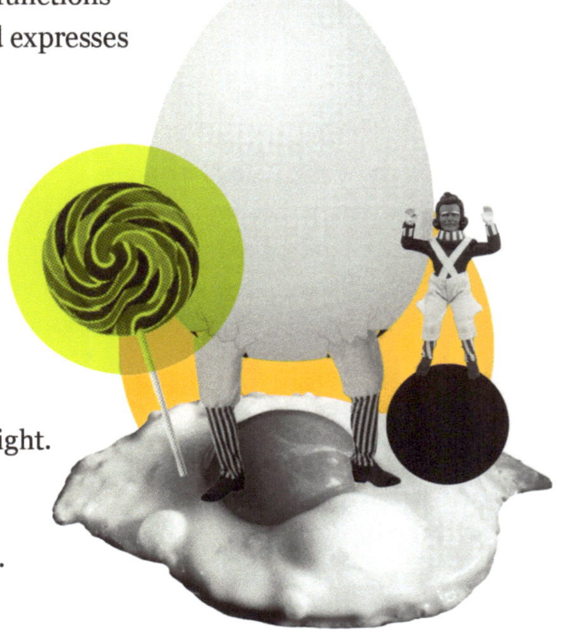

Your Writing Ritual:
▸ Stand with your feet shoulder-width apart.
▸ Clasp your hands overhead and lean gently to the right.
▸ Inhale into the left side of your body.
▸ Exhale and return to center, then repeat to the left.
▸ Do this side-stretch breath cycle twice on each side.
▸ Release your arms and gently roll your neck.

Set your timer for 2 mins.
Answer the following question.
What did you last prepare in the kitchen?

Activity One:
Set your timer for 1 min.
Make a big list of verbs. Examples: fodder / rummage / climb / jiggle

Activity Two:
Set your timer for 2 mins.
Make a list of things you enjoy eating. Examples: lasagna / phở / bacon / moussaka

Activity Three:
Set your timer for 2 mins.
For each of the things you like to eat from [Activity Two], write down a verb that comes to mind
for that food. Examples: lasagna–bubbles / phở–slurp / bacon–sizzle / moussaka–melt

Endurance Writing Prompt:
Set your timer for 15 mins.
You're salivating at the mouth thinking about all the delicious foods you enjoy eating, but you have
none of these dishes on hand. You're in a realm of desire and imagination, and only a poem will satisfy
your hunger. Write a poem, using whatever poetic rules you feel like, to describe the things you love to
eat [Activity Two]. Channel your inner Roald Dahl to play around with verbs both associated [Activity One
and Activity Three] and not associated with these foods to depict food in more ways than just consumption.

Guiding Questions:
What does the texture of your favorite food bring to mind?
How can you reimagine the preparation of a meal using various word associations?

Pre - Dawn

Baby dinosaur yawn.
A meteor of dew down the backbone.
Grains ground between upper and lower
molars.
Deep breath in—
long neck stretched to the sky.
Waking from prehistoric burnout,
stars drawn

down,

down,

down,

through expanded lungs.
Take one Tyrannosaurus rib;
bring me Eve.
Womankind rushes the clock.
I look forward to meeting her in the wind.
If I flew away today, my wings would
glisten teal,
ridged with scales.

Take my offering;
churn out another language.
Spit up love—
for we paint under the same moon.

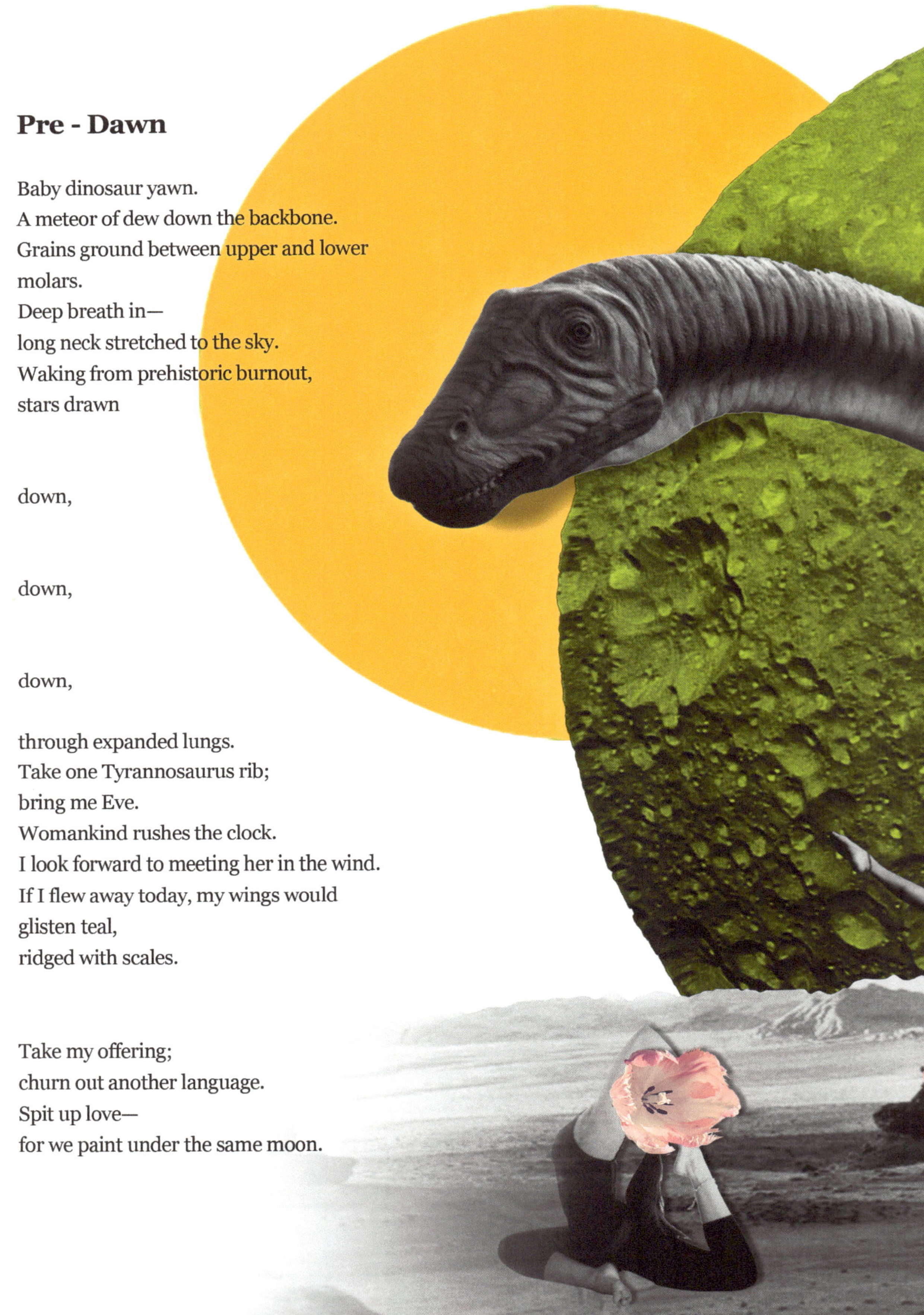

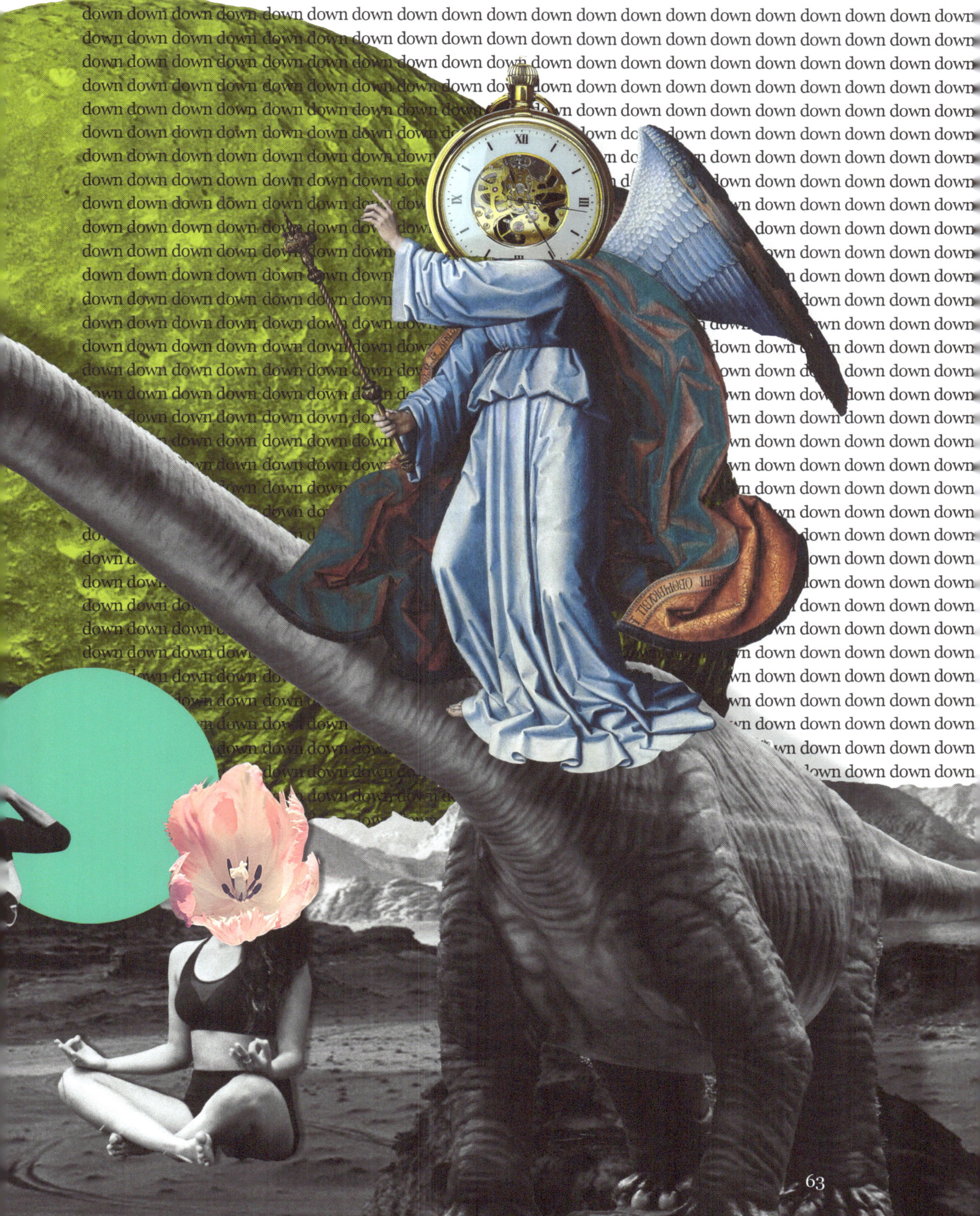

down down down down down down down down down down down down down down down down down down down

Death Dates

My father's pancreatic cancer diagnosis came packed with a timeline. As a family, we navigated each day with the tether of a countdown. On one hand, a gift, as if to see the sand fall through the hourglass. An invitation to take in all of my father's quirky attributes, to listen, to hold him as if we might lose him in the quiet of the night. On the other hand, a curse, no matter of money or alteration in habit, could reverse the clock.

For my father, would ignorance have been a relief? Maybe an extension of his life? Without a timeline, would he have willed to exist in defiance of his cancer? I will never know. We are all fated for an end, perhaps, a blessing, most of us move forward without knowing when our day will come.

In writing, with boundless landscape to ponder, we can explore, test, and play against the partnership of life and death. We can leverage death to heighten plot, to hold some characters hostage to fate, and to enlighten others. On the vast plain of narrative, death roams in many forms. Death can be a narrator, as in *The Book Thief*. Death can be objectified as in *The Picture of Dorian Grey*. Death can be a presence, a twisting puppeteer as in *The Immortalists*. An author understands the mega and the meta of what drives all living beings—to exist. The wrench in these stories, death, relinquishes each protagonist of their ignorance. We experience the vice, the manipulation, or the current of confronting death.

In today's exercise, let's explore fictional stories of characters who know their exact death date.

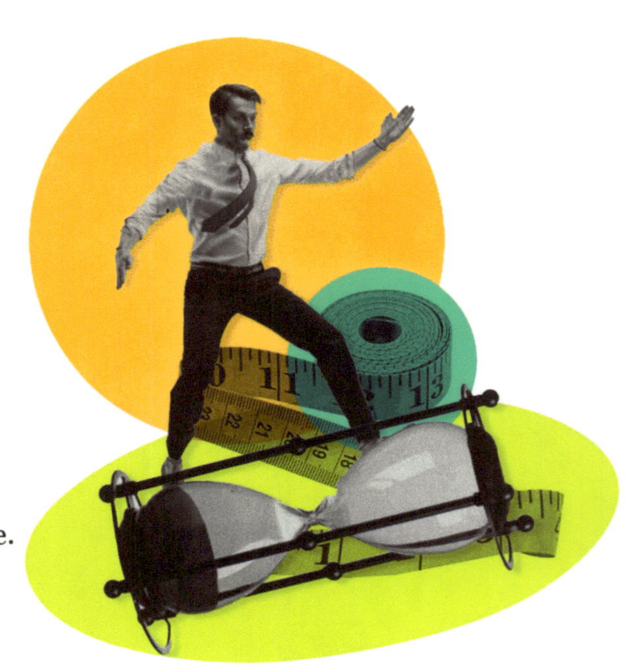

Set Your Intention For Today's Writing Practice

Your Writing Ritual:

- ▶ Stand or sit tall.
- ▶ Gently tap your chest with your fingertips.
- ▶ Breathe in and out slowly.
- ▶ Tap up and down your sternum as you breathe.
- ▶ Continue tapping for three breath cycles.
- ▶ Pause, inhale deeply.
- ▶ Exhale and drop your arms.

Set your timer for 2 mins.
Answer the following question.
How do you prefer to hear bad news?

Activity One:
Set your timer for 2 mins.
Make a list of ways someone might receive prophetic advice. Examples: oracle / tea leaf reading / tarot cards / fortune cookie

Activity Two:
Set your timer for 2 mins.
Make a list of ways a fictional character might try and prove their immortality.
Examples: jumping off a cliff / sky diving without a parachute / poison / walking through flames

Activity Three:
Set your timer for 2 mins.
Make a list of actions a fictional character might take if they knew their death date.
Examples: travel the world / abundance of drugs / sexual escapades / write love letters

Activity Four:
Select one prophetic happening from [Activity One].

Endurance Writing Prompt:
Set your timer for 15 mins.
Write a fictional story where your character is given their exact death date by [Activity Four]. They are convinced of the reading after they test the limits of their immortality [Activity Two]. They live their life in extreme [Activity Three]. Give us their feelings, thoughts, emotions, and beliefs as they arrive at the day they will meet their death.

Guiding Questions:
What actions did your character take to test the theory of their death date?
How does your character shift from before knowing their death date and the date approaching?

The Absence Of Fluff

Reading a block of text, like looking at a well-crafted medieval castle, one can dismiss the individual stones pulling the ensemble together. However, one uneven stone alters the building. One wasted word in your text alters the work. Good writing allows the reader to move through text without tripping on any uneven stones. More than the proverbial one foot in front of the other, good writing is the absence of fluff. Or as Hemingway put it, "All you have to do is write one true sentence. Write the truest sentence that you know."[21]

A good writer allows themselves to play with each sentence, scalpel the fat, and examine if the ideas transcend the page. Readers will skim where you, as the writer, have forfeited the gumption to speak beyond shallow sentences. As Professor Helen Sword insists, "far too many writers send their best ideas out into the world on brittle-boned sentences weighted down with rhetorical flab."[59]

More is not synonymous with better. Pad your prose and you'll lose your frame. Good writing means being daring enough to cut, tweak, alter, and upgrade your sentences. Your voice is truth enough.

In today's exercise, let's write personal statements absent any fluff.

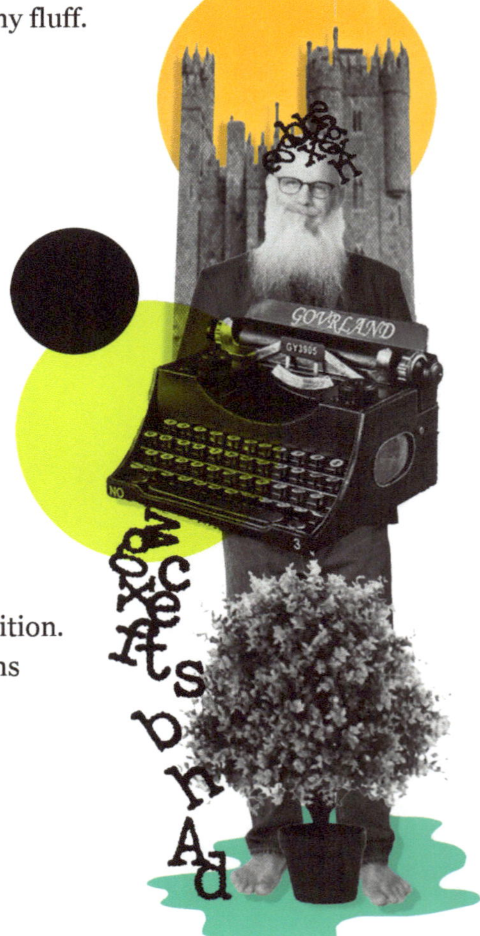

Set Your Intentions For Today's Writing Practice

Your Writing Ritual:

▶ Stand or place your feet flat on the floor from a seated position.
▶ Draw in your breath through your nose and raise your arms above your head.
▶ Hold for three seconds.
▶ Let out your breath in a sigh while dropping your arms down to the floor.
▶ Repeat this cycle five times.
▶ Shake out your arms and wiggle your fingers.

Your Warm-Up:
Set your timer for 2 mins.
Answer the following question.
How do you introduce yourself at a party?

Activity One:
Set your timer for 2 mins.
Make a list of attributes to describe yourself to a group of strangers. Examples: I am 5'3. / I read at bedtime. / I write for work. / My favorite color is green.

Activity Two:
Set your timer for 2 mins.
Make a list of attributes that you would use to elaborate on who you are to people you trust. Examples: I bungee-jumped topless in Peru. / I sing rap in the shower. / I read tarot cards before making a big decision. / Cheese makes me gassy.

Activity Three:
Set your timer for 2 mins.
Make a list of things that you don't like. Examples: touching wet paper towels / confrontation / heavy metal music / deep ocean

Endurance Writing Prompt Part One:
Set your timer for 7 mins.
Imagine you are introducing yourself as a character. Write a first draft introduction of who you are using ideas from [Activity One], [Activity Two], and [Activity Three].

Endurance Writing Prompt Part Two:
Set your timer for 2 mins.
Circle the conjunctions in your draft (and, or, but, so).
Underline all of your verbs (action words).

Endurance Writing Prompt Part Three:
Set your timer for 6 mins.
Rewrite your second draft introduction. Eliminate unnecessary conjunctions and upgrade stale verbs.

Guiding Questions:
Where can you upgrade "to be" verbs in your text: am, are, is, was, were?
If no one read your introduction, what would you be bold enough to write?

Striptease Mishap

I have run this exercise several times in very different cultures, including once in Vietnam and once in Morocco. Spoiler, the exercise calls on the reader to bring strippers into the center of a fictional story. Each time I hold space for what might be uncomfortable, and lead the group through the exercise to detach from their personal opinion on the subject.

I run this exercise with Margaret Atwood in the back of my mind. As Atwood says in *Negotiating With The Dead: A Writer On Writing*, there is "the person who exists when no writing is going forward - the one who washes the floor, eats bran for regularity, takes the car in to be washed, and so forth - and that other, more shadowy and altogether more equivocal personage who shares the same body, and who, when no one is looking, takes it over and uses it to commit the actual writing."[2]

As is with workshop themes gracing taboo, often I can see this proverbial shadowy takeover among writers. Their body language shifts from the initial introduction of the theme to the reading of their work as if a more equivocal persona steps in, allowing them to be artists no matter the subject.

When you can detach art from ownership, the words to follow have free rein to be stark, abrasive, titillating, shocking, easy, gentle, or alluring without consequences of judgment. That's art working at its highest level.

In today's exercise, let's explore writing fiction about the profession of stripping.

Set Your Intention For Today's Writing Practice

Your Writing Ritual:

- Stand or place your feet flat on the floor.
- Extend your arms up and draw in a breath through your nose.
- Drop your arms as you exhale through your mouth.
- Repeat the cycle of reach, inhale, drop, exhale ten times.
- Drop your arms to your side.
- Shake out your hands.

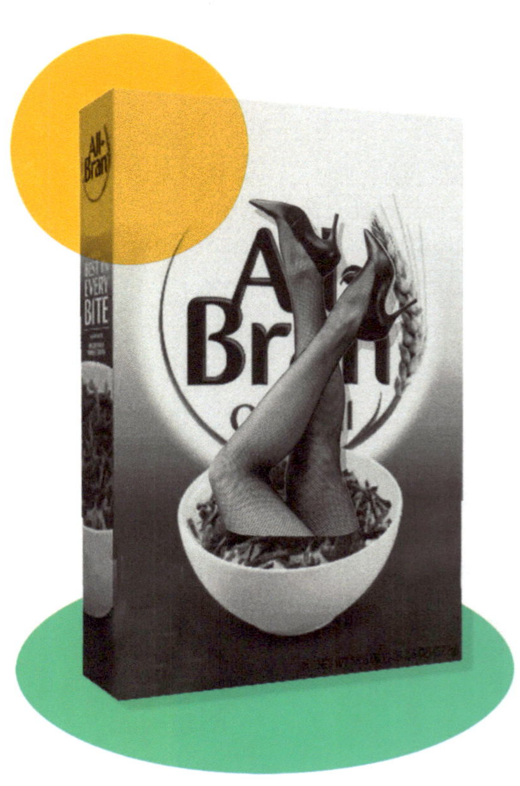

Your Warm-Up:

Set your timer for 2 mins.
Answer the following question.
When was the last time you were in a truly awkward situation?

Activity One:

Set your timer for 2 mins.
Make a bulleted list of fictional male and female stripper names. Examples: Steamy / Dark Horse / Bubbles / Fire

Activity Two:

Set your timer for 2 mins.
Make a bulleted list of things you would absolutely not want to see or not expect to happen at a strip club.
Examples: mom shows up / a man reciting poetry in nothing but a bow tie / you have a history with the
stripper who's been paid to give you a private dance / ping-pong balls are part of the act

Activity Three:

Set your timer for 2 mins.
Make a bulleted list of costumes or outfits a stripper might wear if they were hired for a private event.
Examples: nurse / scientist / teacher / garbage man

Activity Four:

Choose a name from [Activity One].

Activity Five:

Choose an event or sight you wouldn't expect from [Activity Two].

Activity Six:

Choose a costume from [Activity Three].

Endurance Writing Prompt:
Set your timer for 15 mins.
Imagine that [Activity Four] has been hired to give you a private striptease wearing [Activity Six].
Things are going well, but not as you expect when [Activity Five] happens. Jump into the scene when
the first item of clothing has been stripped, dropped, and falls in front of your character.

Guiding Questions:
What is going through your character's head? Can we get a monologue?
How will they handle the event that happens as more clothes come off?

The George Conundrum

For two years, I noticed a pattern in the naming of my characters. My male characters all emerged in the first draft of my work as George. George was the name my grandfather gave everyone in the years he suffered from Alzheimer's. My grandmother, my mother, my father, my brothers, and I were all George.

In the same vein, George became an all-encompassing character for me. The George conundrum had me wondering how other writers work through naming their characters. In a circle of peers, there were two sides of this argument: either firmly believing that their character names define everything about who they are, or the names are fairly dismissible, easily adaptable. Of course, then you have many authors who avoid names altogether for various reasons.

Charles Dickens, the author of classic works like *Great Expectations*, *Hard Times*, and *A Christmas Carol*, had a more forward way of naming his characters. Dickens deployed aptronym as a way to hint to his readers a character's nature. Attributes of his characters made up their last name. Like Mr. Gradgrind, who is obsessed with the graduation of his pupils, which can only be achieved through the grind of study. Other authors, like Suzanne Collins, *The Hunger Games*, touch on similar character naming themes: Katniss is quick, feisty, independent, resilient, like a cat, counter to her more delicate, malleable, and vulnerable sister, Prim. Disney also takes on aspects of aptronym in tales like *Snow White*, where each dwarf embodies their core nature (Sleepy, Sneezy, Dopey, Happy). Characters take on full identities through stories, and a name can make all the difference to your reader.

In today's exercise, let's experiment with character identities to create fictional names.

Definition:
▸ Aptronym: a character's name reflecting his or her personality or dominant traits; a person's name that is regarded as amusingly appropriate to their occupation.

Set Your Intention For Today's Writing Practice

Your Writing Ritual:
▸ Stand or place your feet flat on the floor.
▸ Stretch and hold your left arm across your body.
▸ Breathe in through your nose to the count of four.
▸ Breathe out through your mouth to the count of five.
▸ Drop your left arm.
▸ Switch arms and repeat this tension-release three times.

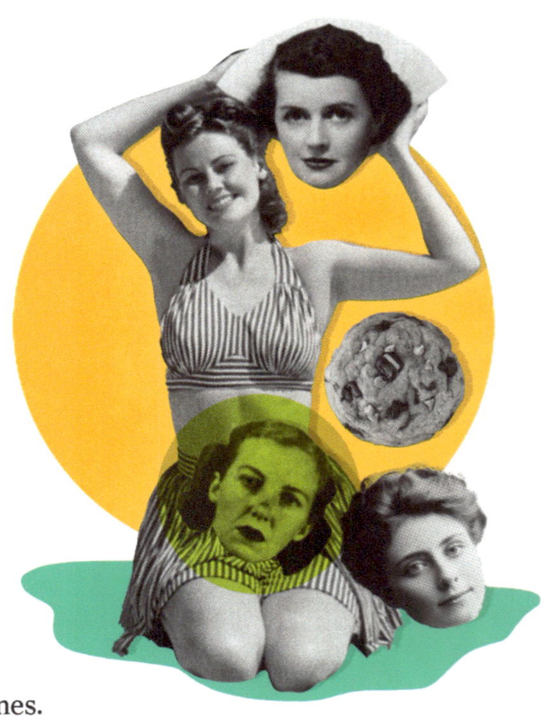

Your Warm-Up:

Set your timer for 2 mins.
Answer the following question.
What was the nickname you wish you had growing up?

Activity One:

Set your timer for 2 mins.
Make a list of all general character types you can think of. Examples: the murderer / the party animal / the snob
/ the tattletale

Activity Two:

Choose one character type from [Activity One] that interests you.

Activity Three:

Set your timer for 2 mins.
Make a general list of wants and desires your character from [Activity Two] might risk everything to get.
Examples: riches / peace & quiet / purpose / the last box on earth of Thin Mint cookies

Activity Four:

Choose one want or desire from [Activity Three].

Activity Five:

Set your timer for 3 mins.
Make a list of character names that describe both your character type and what they desire most in the world.
Examples for the hero who wants peace & quiet: Captain Zen / Lady Shush / Cool Jets / Dr. Peace Primer

Activity Six:

Choose a name from [Activity Five].

Endurance Writing Prompt:
Set your timer for 15 mins.
Write a scene in first person where your character type [Activity Two] introduces themselves to the
reader for the first time. Begin with their name [Activity Six]. Use the first person to give us an inner
monologue about how this character sees the world. Take us through a typical day in their life using
events or scenarios as clues for what they desire most in the world [Activity Four].

Guiding Questions:
How would your character act if told they would never get what they wanted?
What is the biggest roadblock in your character getting what they want?

Nightmares

Toni Morrison is one of the greatest writers of the 21st century. As a Nobel Prize winner and beloved professor at some of the most prestigious universities in the world, she wrote the most brutal fiction I've ever read. Fiction that I could not put down. Tales of racism, sexism, and classism spun from nodes in a shared history mark her work as rich and repulsive. Novels like *The Bluest Eye, Paradise, Love,* and *Beloved* are all chisels in the facade of equality for people of color in America's past and present history. Morrison advocated for truth through her pen.

"This is the time for every artist in every genre to do what he or she does loudly and consistently. It doesn't matter to me what your position is. You've got to keep asserting the complexity and the originality of life, and the multiplicity of it, and the facets of it. This is about being a complex human being in the world, not about finding a villain."[38]

Writing, even fiction, is a form of truth we need at times to address nightmarish realities—the complexities and facets of life. Truths about genocide, hate, pain, and suffering benefit from a literary lens to be palatable. Honing in on the nightmares within society is another way to hold a microscope to the world around us. We can use writing to speak, to reflect, to find clarity in matters of terror. We can use expression to flex against the weight of the world.

In today's exercise, let's unpack through writing the realities of the world that give us nightmares.

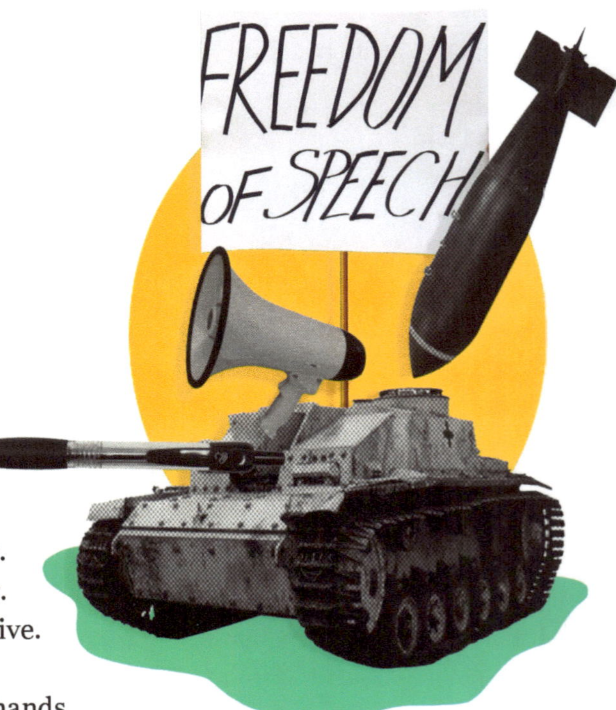

Set Your Intention For Today's Writing Practice

Your Writing Ritual:
- Stand or sit with your feet flat on the floor.
- Interlace your fingers so that your palms face out.
- Breathe in through your nose to the count of four.
- Breathe out through your mouth to the count of five.
- Repeat your breathing four times.
- Drop your arms to your side and shake out your hands.

Your Warm-Up:
Set your timer for 2 mins.
Answer the following question.
What issue would you solve in the world with the press of a magic button?

Activity One:
Set your timer for 2 mins.
Make a list of events, injustices, standards, or horrors about the world that might keep you up at night.
Examples: malnourished children / gun violence / inequitable education / silence

Activity Two:
Pick one event, injustice, standard, or horror from [Activity One].

Activity Three:
Set your timer for 2 mins.
Based on what you picked in [Activity Two], jot down a list of things you know to be true about the event, injustice, standard, or horror. Examples for gun violence: You are more likely to shoot someone if you have a gun than if you don't have a gun. / Gun violence in schools is a problem that primarily exists in the US. / Guns are a want, not a need. / Police forces in the UK do not carry guns.

Activity Four:
Set your timer for 2 mins.
Make a list of words you would associate with the event, injustice, standard, or horror.
Examples for gun violence: repulsed / savage / heat / helpless

Endurance Writing Prompt:
Set your timer for 15 mins.
Write a reactionary poem about the event, injustice, or horror from [Activity Two]. Use the words from [Activity Four] to inspire the first word of new sentences. Use truths from [Activity Three] to lift your writing and make a statement.

Guiding Questions:
Where do you see this event, injustice, or horror taking place in the world?
Why does this feel relevant to you today?

Six Heavy Words

Hemingway, the master of brevity, is legend to have championed a short story of six words. "For sale: baby shoes, never worn."[10] In these six words, there is a story beneath the surface, an iceberg submerged, unseen under the water. The six words of his story contain the necessary elements for a story: a character (the seller of the shoes) who has a desire driving the story (to discard the never worn shoes) and a conflict (something that caused the baby shoes to never be worn).

Hemingway's stylistic preferences push the reader to do the heavy lifting to uncover the story, or rather, build their own story. There is a quest, a need to view and review the spaces between words for something deeper. Why does our character need to sell the shoes vs. throw them away or donate them? What manner of ill fate or change of heart left the tiny shoes empty, unused? Hemingway leaves us, as the reader, to deduce our own conclusions. Beautifully, his brevity encourages readers to build their own long-form narrative to answer all his unanswered questions.

Similar to the Hemingway style—brief, direct, declarative—social media apps have conditioned writers to share their thoughts in concise format. Our current age of character counting and clickbait headlines echoes Hemingway's effort to stir curiosity, to let the reader do the heavy lifting. Writers challenging themselves to brevity must court their readers in a dance of linguistic verbosity and taut direction.

In today's exercise, let's explore brevity in a modern-day concept by writing stories of only six words.

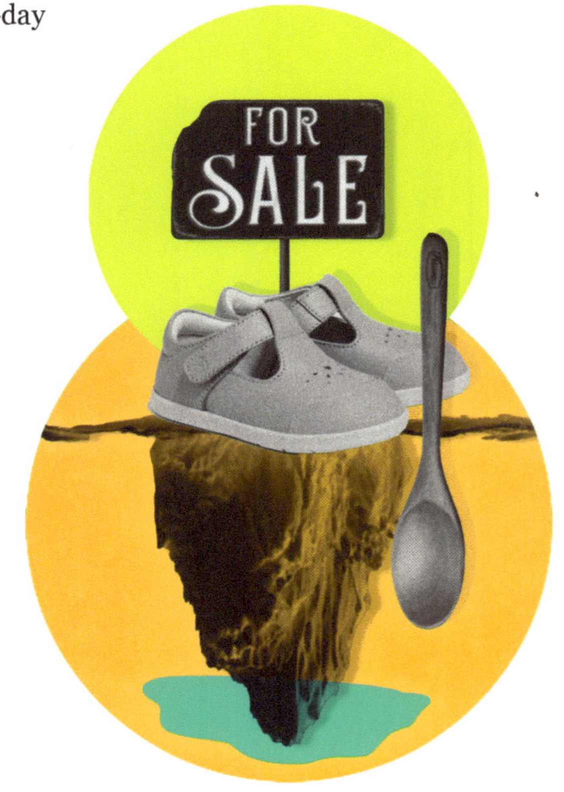

Set Your Intention For Today's Writing Practice

Your Writing Ritual:

► Sit comfortably and bring awareness to your jaw.
► Inhale through your nose.
► Exhale and let your mouth hang open slightly, relaxing your jaw.
► Gently wiggle your jaw side to side.
► Repeat this breath and movement five times.
► Roll your shoulders and relax your arms.

Set your timer for 2 mins.
Answer the following question.
Where did you wake up this morning?

Activity One:
Choose an emotion to build a six-word story around today. Examples: revenge / bliss / fear / regret

Activity Two:
Set your timer for 2 mins.
For someone in a state of emotion [Activity One], make a list of what someone feeling this emotion would want most in the world. Examples for revenge: public embarrassment of their nemesis / righteous action / justice / a personal apology

Activity Three:
Choose one want from your list in [Activity Two].

Activity Four:
Set your timer for 1 min.
Based on the secret selected in [Activity Three], make a list of reasons why someone might feel they could never share their secret. Example for I whistle when I pee: I would die of embarrassment if my boss knew. / I would have to change up my tune if others knew. / My a cappella group would discover I'm tone deaf if they knew. / My therapist would suspect I'm not getting better if she knew.

Activity Five:
Choose one need from your list in [Activity Four].

Activity Six:
Set your timer for 1 min.
For someone in a state of emotion [Activity One] who needs something from others [Activity Five] to get the thing they most want in the world [Activity Three], make a list of what they can give in exchange.
Examples for revenge: money / a letter of recommendation / laundry service for a week / gym membership

Endurance Writing Prompt:
Set your timer for 15 mins.
Use the structure you've already begun to build to write a social media post. Challenge yourself to ask something of your viewers [Activity Five] and what they get in exchange [Activity Six] without overexploiting what it is your character wants most in the world. Withhold the why of the exchange [Activity Three] to create the iceberg effect. Remember, your story is grounded in a feeling of [Activity One]. Rework the want as your iceberg, and the exchange between your character and the audience as the tip of the iceberg.

Guiding Questions:
If you had to whisper the "ask" in a secret meeting, what would you leave out?
How does changing the "ask" from your audience change the tone of your post?

The Tank Is On E

Escaping Casablanca, Morocco, to the seaside for a week, I was seeking silence, or so I thought. My usual days are filled with typing in a home office behind a glass sliding door facing the surge of traffic. My space is smothered by the city's need to belch, a body active in digesting the movement of her 10.5 million dwellers.

I believed that I had left the city in search of silence, the absence of all noise, but nestled in a blanket under the sunset, I was struck by the obvious fact that to have the privilege to hear is to notice the world is always breathing. Even in the depths of the desert or in a soundproof studio, there is something moving, working, creating friction, and jostling atoms to make sound.

We require an awareness of movement in the world to bring something to the blank page as writers, to tackle the feigned idea of writer's block. As author Anne Lamott offers in her novel *Bird By Bird*, writers are not blocked. "The word block suggests that you are constipated or stuck, when the truth is that you're empty."[32]

Go fill up on the world and all of its noise. Notice the world tiptoeing, the hum-drum of the city, the brush of ferns and flowers in the wind, the hum of birds' beating wings, and the distant muffle of conversation. In writing, there is a temptation to rely heavily on sight. Images are quick, but pulling the reader through the page and into the story takes a full sensory experience.

In today's exercise, let's ground ourselves in using sound as a way to describe the world.

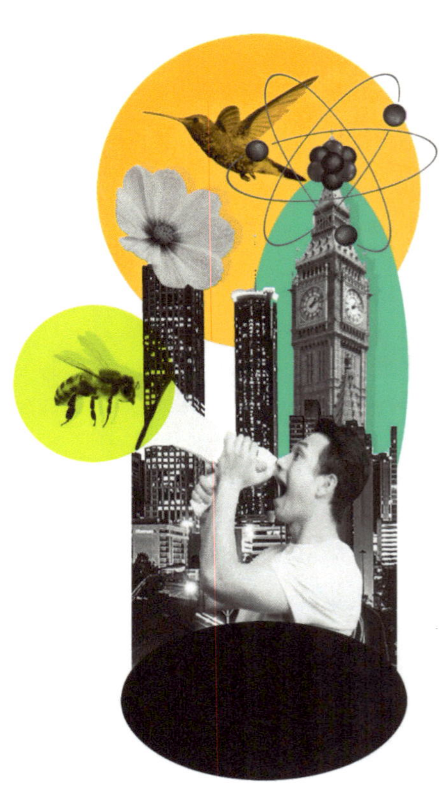

Set Your Intentions For Today's Writing Practice

Your Writing Ritual:

- Sit or stand with your arms relaxed.
- Lift your arms out to the side and bend your elbows to form a cactus shape.
- Inhale and draw your shoulder blades together.
- Exhale and relax your chest.
- Repeat this movement for five breath cycles.
- Release your arms and shake them out.

Set your timer for 2 mins.
Answer the following question.
What is the first sound you hear in the morning?

Activity One:
Set your timer for 2 mins.
Make a list of all the sounds and noises you can hear in your environment. Examples: the wheeze of my dog snoring / the farts of an old motorcycle idling outside / the hum of my computer overheating / the creak of the floorboards upstairs

Activity Two:
Set your timer for 2 mins.
Make a list of sounds that bring a smile to your face. Examples: the high-hat in jazz / when my dog yawns / the FaceTime ringtone / the crunch of snow under tires after the sun goes down

Activity Three:
Choose one sound from your list created in [Activity One or Two].

Endurance Writing Prompt:
Set your timer for 15 mins.
Take this session to write about your chosen sound [Activity Three]. Give the sound dimension beyond your ears. Explore other similar sounds. Venture to guess how this sound is made and the components as part of the noises you hear. Allow your pen to flow in creating the sound for your reader.

Guiding Questions:
How does your body react when hearing this sound?
What would happen if this sound disappeared? Or if it were intensified?

On The Chopping Block

The English language contains more than a hundred thousand verbs. A mass that should diversify the page, but for the sake of quick function, writers default to familiar verbs. Helen Sword, professor and trained Literary Scholar in Auckland, writes, "active verbs such as grow, fling and exhale infuse your writing with vigor and metaphorical zing; they put legs on your prose." She further iterates how writing with the use of the be verbs – am, are, is, was, were – is an easier way to write, but they "carry you nowhere."[60]

Overhauling verbs in our work is a corrective action, but as writers, it's ideal to build the habit of varied vocabulary when we're on deck to write. Natalie Goldberg outlines one of my favorite exercises for building creative muscles around varied word choice. In her book *Writing Down The Bones*, she has writers match verbs attributed to a profession (like cooking) with abstract nouns. She challenges writers to create stronger images, pairing abstract nouns and verbs. In the book, her method made a playful dynamic of cooking verbs as a way to serve up new sentences in your writing.

Both Sword and Goldberg believe your writing benefits from motion. The heat beneath savory writing is varied verbs. Descriptions permeate the air when dressed well. You can sauté plot with precise verbs. Verbs season your sentence, flavoring day-old dishes of yesterday's writing to instead be Michelin star garnished sentences we salivate to read.

In today's exercise, let's pepper in cooking verbs to describe a day in the life.

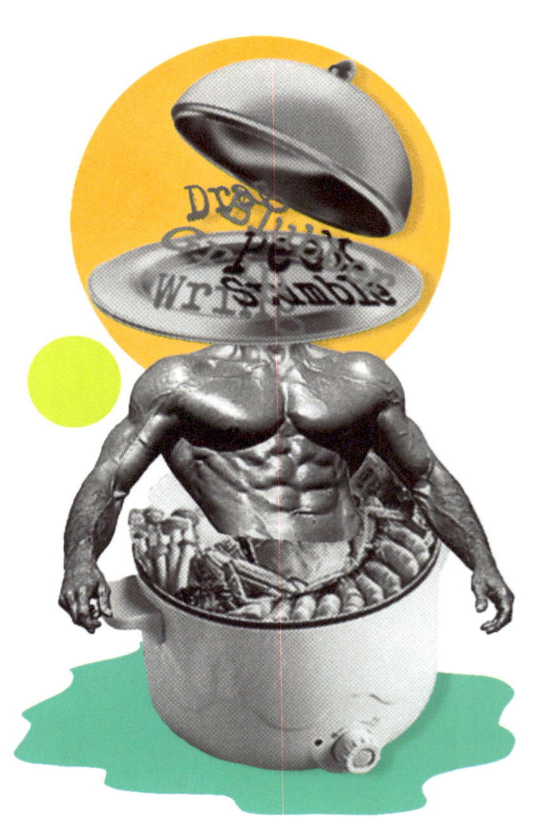

Set Your Intention For Today's Writing Practice

Your Writing Ritual:

▸ Sit with your hands resting on your thighs.
▸ Inhale slowly through your nose.
▸ Breathe into your abdomen instead of your chest.
▸ Exhale with a soft "shhhh" sound.
▸ Repeat six times.
▸ Stretch your arms overhead and release.

Your Warm-Up:
Set your timer for 2 mins.
Answer the following question.
How do you feel about work on Mondays?

Activity One:
Set your timer for 3 mins.
Make a list of verbs associated with the profession of cooking. Examples: seer / marinate / filet / shuck

Activity Two:
Set your timer for 2 mins.
Make a list of different professions. Examples: consultant / customer support representative / waitress / mechanic

Activity Three:
Pick a profession from [Activity Two].

Activity Four:
Drawing from the profession picked in [Activity Three], make a list of tasks a person in that profession might cover any given day on the job. Examples for mechanic: make assessments / change oil / replace parts / lubricate pistons

Endurance Writing Prompt:
Set your timer for 15 mins.
Create a day in the life of a fictional character. Start by imagining it's Monday morning for your fictional character as a [Activity Three]. They've arrived at work for yet another day on the job. Set the scene for our reader. Convey how our character feels about their job using cooking verbs from [Activity One] to describe their role, their routine, their atmosphere at work.

Guiding Questions:
Who do they encounter throughout their Monday?
What motivates your character to come to work, yes, even on Mondays?

Second Hand Gems

The novel *Holes*, by Louis Sachar, is a story of mysticism, curses, desert quests, and onion-eating lizards. The tale kicks off with a stolen pair of sneakers. Our two fated characters end up in a correctional camp for troubled youth. The one, Stanley, pegged for stealing the sneakers on auction to raise money for a homeless shelter. The other, Zero, the true thief. Zero tells Stanley he hadn't been able to read the sign at the auction. He felt it was better to steal a used pair of shoes than a new pair.

Underneath the heavier themes of rejection, classism, homelessness, and justice, we find innocence. Zero's a kid with a big dream to change his circumstances. The author's choice to use shoes as the focal point is intentional. On the surface, one might garner a cautionary message of perspective, to walk in someone else's shoes—momentairly waning to empathy. What happens if, instead, as Zero had hoped, a pair of shoes could permanently change his circumstances? What if footwear upgrades held the possibility of magic, like in the novel *Someone Else's Shoes* and the children's book *Juno Valentine and the Magical Shoes*? Shoes are one of many ways a writer can echo the belief that we may change our fate by way of what we wear.

As Louis Sachar does in *Holes*, we can draw attention to desire or despair. We can create complex characters whose hopes hinge on an everyday object like the right pair of shoes. Whether we are privileged to dazzle ourselves in the finest footwear or cap our feet in second hand gems, a pair of shoes can carry a story just as they carry us.

In today's exercise, let's write a narrative of your life by exploring the history of your shoes.

Set Your Intentiuon For Today's Writing Practice

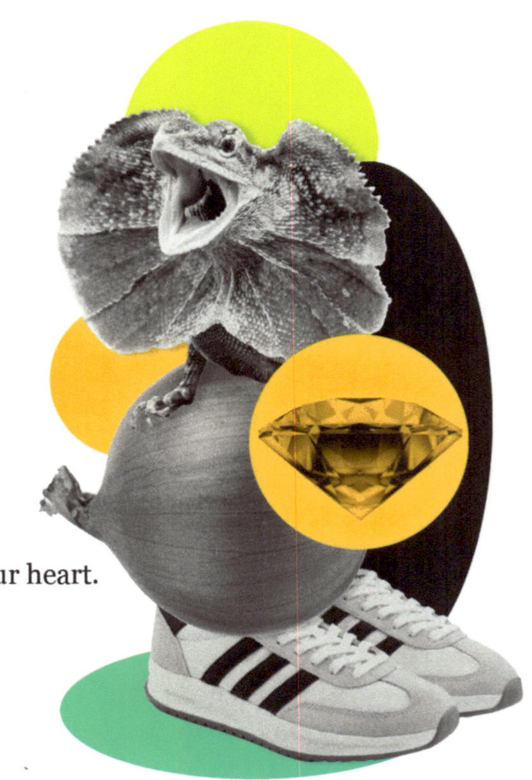

Your Writing Ritual:

- ▶ Sit or stand with a straight back.
- ▶ Place one hand behind your neck and the other on your heart.
- ▶ Inhale and lengthen your spine.
- ▶ Exhale and imagine tension melting from your neck.
- ▶ Hold this posture for three full breaths.
- ▶ Switch hands and repeat.

Set your timer for 2 mins.
Answer the following question.
How do you feel about wearing shoes?

Activity One:
Set your timer for 1 min.
Make a list of all the types of footwear you can think of. Examples: sandals / go-go boots / flippers / sneakers

Activity Two:
Set your timer for 2 mins.
Jot down some notes about how it feels to wear a good pair of shoes. Think about how you walk in them, how they carry you, what you can conquer, or why they feel spectacular.

Activity Three:
Set your timer for 1 min.
Drawing from your past, jot down as much as you can remember when you think of shoes from your childhood.

Activity Four:
Set your timer for 1 min.
Drawing from your past, jot down as much as you can remember when you think of shoes from your adolescent years.

Activity Five:
Set your timer for 1 min.
Drawing from your present, jot down as much as you can when you think of shoes in your present life.

Endurance Writing Prompt:
Set your timer for 15 mins.
You have loose ideas about the theme of shoes from three different periods in your life—childhood, adolescence, and the present. It's time to string those ideas into a stream of conscious narrative about shoes—the stories they tell, the energy they carry, the memories they hold or don't hold. Create a short narrative of all you can remember about the many pairs of shoes in your life.

Guiding Questions:
Who bought you your favorite pair of shoes?
Which shoes made you feel the most confident, and which made you feel the most shame?

Postcard Confessions

In 2013, my best friend, Elle, and I joined a postcard platform in college called Postcrossing. As such, we received postcards from strangers around the world in a 1:1 exchange. No return address. Just a written code to log a postcard's arrival on your online profile. Mostly, I joined the site with an interest in world stamps.

Out of the 14 postcards I received that year, one remains potent in my mind a decade later. Olga, a 39-year-old language teacher, wrote to me from Belarus. Her first two sentences were declarative, simple, haunting. Without a return address, the words were an untraceable whisper that I read like a woman writing from a high castle with a beautiful and unattainable view. In the total absence of knowing one another, she wrote that life in Belarus was unbearable. She wished to be anywhere else. She wished to live a life of fashion, art, New York, and horses. There were no questions, simply what landed as a confession. Her honesty still gives me goosebumps.

Without hyperbole, Olga risked jail time to speak against her country. Badmouthing Belarus is a crime punishable by up to two years in jail. She risked this to write in English to a complete stranger. If I had been wiser in my twenties, more empathetic and well-traveled, I would have found a way to write back, to mirror her honesty. I would have used every bit of white space to break the topic of politeness and show up as human. When I log into the Postcrossing platform now, her profile reads "last seen over 10 years ago." I am left to wonder.

Olga reminds me that when we write with honesty, the reader can feel the difference. Author Ray Bradbury backs up this feeling as he wrote, "in quickness is truth. The faster you blurt, the more swiftly you write, the more honest you are."[4]

What is quicker and more swift than a postcard? Reduced to the 3 x 4 inches of white space, we can detail only so much of a journey or try to capture a place. We can break expectations, trim the fat of wasted words, to dive into a deeper part of ourselves to connect with our reader.

In today's exercise, let's explore writing with more honesty through fictional pen pal confessions.

Set Your Intention For Today's Writing Practice.

Your Writing Ritual:

▶ Stand with your feet hip-width apart.
▶ Inhale while drawing circles with your hips clockwise.
▶ Exhale as you reverse the direction.
▶ Continue for four breath cycles.
▶ Stand tall and stretch your arms upward.
▶ Drop your arms and shake out your hands.

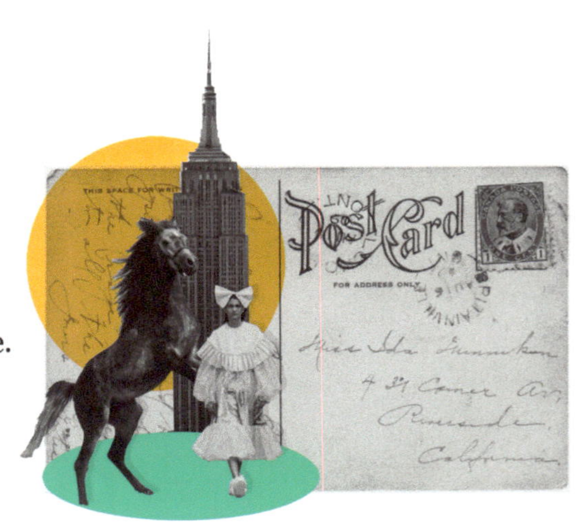

Your Warm-Up:

Set your timer for 2 mins.
Answer the following question.
Who was your pen pal in school?

Activity One:

Set your timer for 2 mins.
Make a list of questions you would expect a pen pal to ask or answer in a letter. Examples: How's the weather? / How's work?/ Any exciting events going on? / What's in your grandmother's goulash recipe?

Activity Two:

Set your timer for 2 mins.
Make a list of secrets you would never write to a stranger. Examples: I whistle when I pee. / Peanut butter makes me gassy. / My spirit animal is a unicorn. / I killed my neighbor's apple tree.

Activity Three:

Choose two secrets from [Activity Two].

Activity Four:

Set your timer for 2 mins.
Based on the secret selected in [Activity Three], make a list of reasons why someone might feel they could never share their secret. Example for I whistle when I pee: I would die of embarrassment if my boss knew. / I would have to change up my tune if others knew. / My a cappella group would discover I'm tone deaf if they knew. / My therapist would suspect I'm not getting better if she knew.

Endurance Writing Prompt:

Set your timer for 15 mins.
Imagine a character that feels alone in their secret. Afterall, the worst would happen [Activity Four] if their secret got out. They've acquired an anonymous pen pal through a new snail mail service. Write a postcard to the pen pal with a few polite sentences [Activity One]. Quickly move into your character confessing their secret [Activity Three].

Guiding Questions:

What would a character hope to gain from confessing a secret to a total stranger?
How would a feeling of being lonely affect your character's letter?

Mealtime Memories

I hired a young Italian language teacher to try and learn Italian during Covid. Andrea was cool-natured and intelligent. I lived in Vietnam at the time, and it was permissible to take lessons in her apartment, where her kitchen doubled as our classroom. As I learned the names for food and how to order, I discovered that it's customary in Italy to have a five-course meal. I found this astonishing as Andrea had the proportions of a model. She assured me that when you're in Italy, meals are savored, not something to be rushed, and your body has a way of making room over time. Two hours might creep by before the closing coffee and Limoncello are served.

I struggled to remember a time I'd spent two hours parsing out a meal around a table with others. I'm one to take breakfast on the go and lunch at my desk. I liked imagining all the ways families in Italy passed the time over food. Where grandmothers insisted their guests eat more, and conversation carried over piping hot lasagna. There's a reason Elizabeth Gilbert's book *Eat, Pray, Love* had a whole section on eating in Italy—comfort is found in your taste buds.

When we think about ways to see the world, food is a powerful medium. People want to share their foodie experiences. Readers need not stretch to imagine the texture, taste, or smell of a good meal. As writers, food is a way to break into the blank page because, as Natalie Goldberg writes, "when it comes to food, people know what they like, are definite, concrete, explicit."[16]

In today's exercise, let's activate our stomach and explore meals as the focal point of memory.

Set Your Intaention For Today's Writing Practice

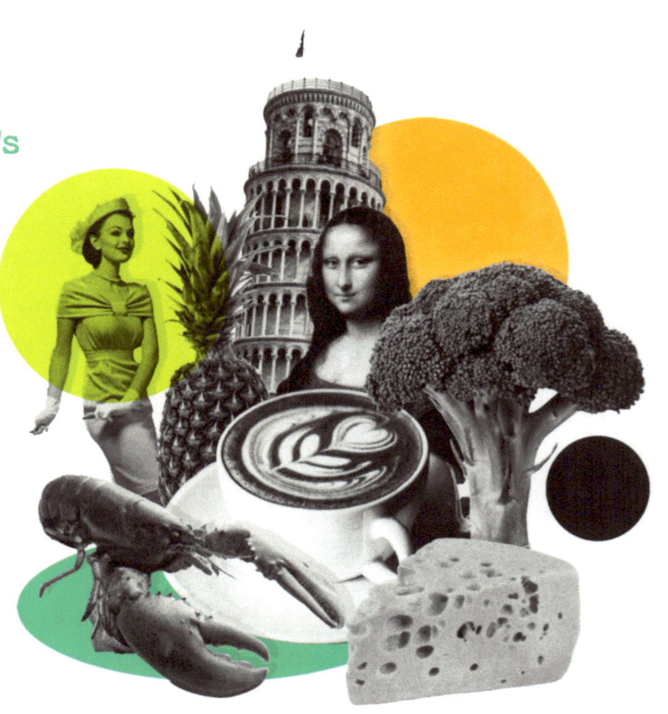

Your Writing Ritual:

- Stand or sit with your spine tall.
- Gently tap the outside of your left arm with your opposite hand.
- Tap from your shoulder down the outside of your arm all the way to the top of your hand.
- Turn up your palm and tap up the inside of your arm back to your shoulder.
- Repeat this cycle three times on each arm.
- Shake out your hands.

Set your timer for 2 mins.
Answer the following question.
What did mealtime look like when you were growing up?

Activity One:
Set your timer for 2 mins.
Make a list of your favorite meals to eat. Examples: my mom's fried chicken and asparagus sauce / green chili-smothered breakfast burritos / Thanksgiving / blueberry pancakes and crispy bacon

Activity Two:
Set your timer for 2 mins.
Make a list of memories from meals that brought you joy. Examples: eggs benedict & lobster with Uncle Bob / curry at La Pacha with Justin and Andrea / Friendsgiving in Da Nang / Christmas with expats on the beach in Nelson

Activity Three:
Choose one meal from [Activity Two].

Activity Four:
Using the focus of the meal chosen in [Activity Three], tap into your five senses to jot down finite details about the meal.

Endurance Writing Prompt:
Set your timer for 15 mins.
Imagine you are given a photograph. The photograph is a significant moment centered around a meal [Activity Three]. The photograph sparks imagery deeper than the picture, drawing upon scents, sounds, and feelings in your gut [Activity Four]. Write as if the reader can see the photograph and can feel the frame come to life with your sensory details.

Guiding Questions:
Who is with you in the photograph?
Who cooked the meal featured in the photograph?

Your EQ Resume

I earned extra cash after university by mentoring third and fourth-year students on the art of resume writing. In a one-hour tutoring session, I broke down the executive summary and layered in steps for excavating expert skills. Even with limited linear professional experience at the time, I knew two things—a resume required a litany of active verbs and a pinch of creativity. No boss is perking up at your dull listicle. This was before AI could offer a nearly polished first draft.

Beefing up resumes sparked the idea of using a technical writing structure as a catalyst for building creative writing muscles. How much could you unearth about a character through a resume? Even better, what if the character was familiar to the writer so that, with a limited runway, they could get right to the meat of a character's history, hopes, weaknesses, and strengths?

Using a resume structure, writers can feed the reader a power-packed history in just a one-page professional brief. Like all writing, when you know the structure, you can rebel against what's expected. You can rotate the rules of writing when you know how the ball joints move.

In today's exercise, let's use the resume structure to craft stories where your emotions are applying for a job.

Set Your Intention For Today's Writing Practice

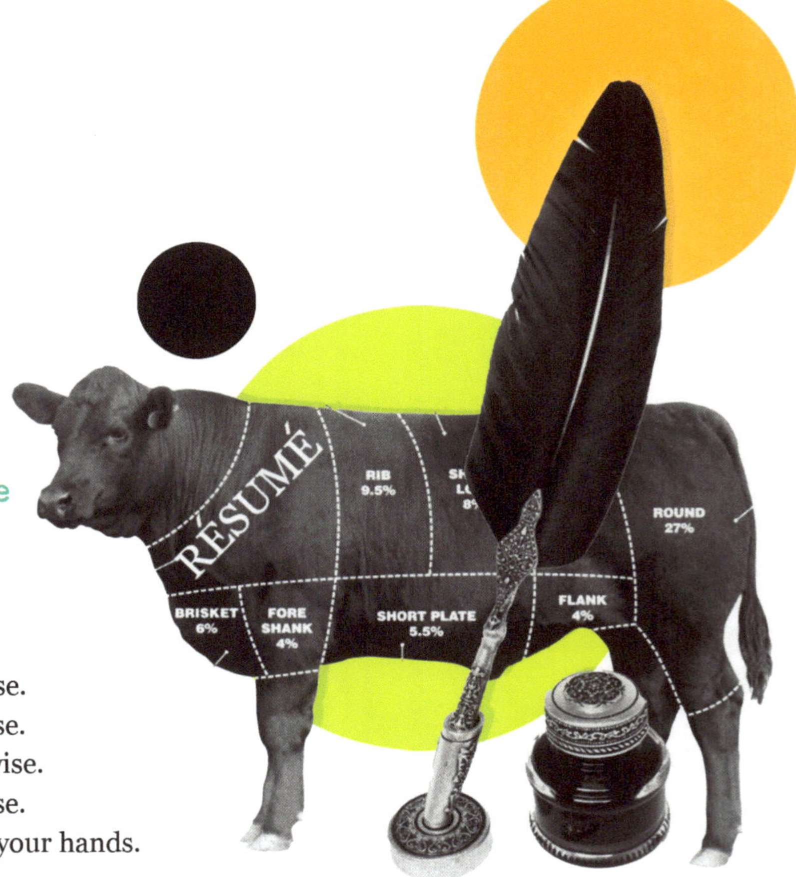

Your Writing Ritual:

► Sit comfortably.
► Rotate your right wrist clockwise.
► After three breath cycles, reverse.
► Switch wrists and rotate clockwise.
► After three breath cycles, reverse.
► Drop your arms and shake out your hands.

Set your timer for 2 mins.
Answer the following question.
What was your first job you needed a resume for?

Activity One:
Set your timer for 2 mins.
Jot down a list of all the times you might feel frustrated, and you have to actively check your emotions.
Examples: stuck in traffic / confrontation at work / partner left the peanut butter jar open and out on the counter / watching the news

Activity Two:
Pick one example of being frustrated from [Activity One].

Activity Three:
Pick one emotion you might lean into if you were in the frustrating situation from [Activity Two].

Activity Four:
Set your timer for 2 mins.
To make the first part of your resume, jot down a list of key skills for how your emotion from [Activity Three], assists or shows up when you're in the situation picked from [Activity Two]. Examples for traffic and anger: provided fiery support to help the driver feel in control of the halted traffic / spoke boisterously foul language to help the driver feel empowered / tensed the muscles of the driver to encourage strength in a still situation / increased levels of adrenaline so the driver had maximum focus in case of danger

Activity Five:
To build credibility for your emotion being the best emotion for the job, jot down a list of past experiences from the emotion's perspective using active verbs. Examples for anger: resolved Wednesday's dispute over the last piece of chicken / rallied in support against the referee's bogus call in the game / raged against the increase in gas prices at the pump / fed the ego when that dude cut in line

Endurance Writing Prompt:
Set your timer for 15 mins.
You're hiring the best emotion to handle the situation of [Activity Two]. Time freezes, and you conduct an emotional interview on how to handle the situation. [Activity Three] has submitted a resume to be highly considered for handling the job. Put together a resume, complete with attributes [Activity Four] and job history [Activity Five] on why the emotion applying for the position is best suited for the job.

Guiding Questions:
What would the emotion want its interviewer to know above all else?
What happens if your emotion is not chosen for the job, and how can you leverage those gaps in a professional summary?

A Doctorate In Living

My husband, Thomas, hosts Trivial Pursuit once a month. What started in college as part of his responsibilities working in the service industry became a sharpened skill deployed in the places we've lived around the world. He is extraordinary at orchestrating a space where, no matter background, age, or level of education, your personal expertise in living is your asset. As the game begins, I love watching individuals scroll through their minds for some clue, an answer to a question on geography or pop culture, a fact about fruit, or the name of the fourth ghost in Pac-Man (Inky? Pinky?). No Google. No phones. No ChatGPT. I love watching each person tap into their own experience. It's a room full of adults who adore the idea of sharing what they know for the prize of writing their team name on a handmade Stanley Cup style trophy constructed from recycled plastic and tinfoil.

I asked to team up with a woman I'd never met for the last trivia I attended. Kathy smiled, shook my hand, and immediately apologized. "I didn't have any answers to the questions last month," she said. As I'd seen numerous times before, Kathy just hadn't hit the right round yet. I thought of *Big Magic* and how Elizabeth Gilbert writes, "trust that the world has been educating you all along... after a certain age, no matter how you've been spending your time, you have very likely earned a doctorate in living."[13]

I told Kathy, "you know more than you think." We teamed up with another first-timer, Jade. Our team took first place. We signed the trophy as The Quizzard of Oz Trio.

I'm reminded that we each have a wealth of experience. Writers pluck from experience to go deeper in making sense of the world. Writing is a place to unpack the unknown, but also a space to expand on the things already digested. Your scholarship in being human on this planet is worth an infinite amount of white space, and it begins with your curiosity. Curiosity is a way to make sense of the world, to study, and to share what we know about what we love, even when convention says we are crazy to do so.

In today's exercise, let's use writing as a way to lean into truth around being scholars of our own lives.

Set Your Intention For Today's Writing Practice

Your Writing Ritual:

► Stand tall or sit up straight with your eyes closed.
► On your inhale, slowly turn your head to the left.
► On your exhale, return your head to the center.
► Inhale and turn your head to the right.
► Exhale and return to the center.
► Repeat this gentle head-turning breath cycle six times.

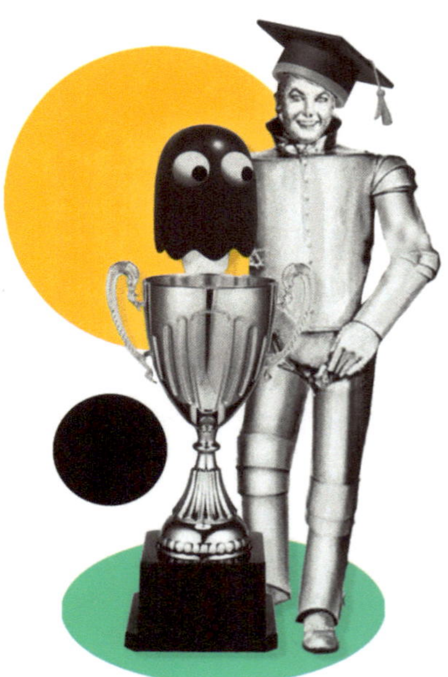

Your Warm-Up:
Set your timer for 2 mins.
Answer the following question.
What was the last subject you deep-dived into researching?

Activity One:
Set your timer for 2 mins.
Make a list of subjects or passions you feel overwhelmingly called to discuss from personal experience.
Examples: writing / travel / dancing in the rain / bacon

Activity Two:
Choose one subject from [Activity One].

Activity Three:
Set your timer for 2 mins.
Make a list of life lessons you've unearthed about your subject from [Activity Two]. Examples for dancing in the rain: spontaneity is key / disregard the itchy feeling after you're done dancing / ignore the reaction of others / do acknowledge the joy in your heart

Activity Four:
Set your timer for 2 mins.
Make a list of who might be a fun audience to share your scholarly lessons on the subject from [Activity Two]. Examples: librarians / first graders / recovering addicts / rodeo clowns

Activity Five:
Choose an audience from [Activity Four].

Endurance Writing Prompt:
Set your timer for 15 mins.
You are the foremost world-renowned scholar on subject matter [Activity Two]. You are asked to write a speech sharing your unearthed life lessons on this subject [Activity Three] with a group of [Activity Five]. Remember, this is your personal experience. There are no wrong answers as you share what you know.

Guiding Questions:
Why does the subject resonate deeply for you?
What is the message you hope your audience takes away from sharing your knowledge?

Freedom

Shackles broken, chains removed, titles given, votes cast—
would Martin Luther King be humbled or horrified by where
we are now? Humans are a continual work in progress.

In a small café across the Atlantic from where my passport
says I belong, sitting among friends peeling back the edges of
oppression, my freedoms are blinding.

To live, to work, to roam without fault or much failure.
To own an identity.
I am a sexual being—a woman fully in touch with pleasure.
Freedom to talk about sex.
To have sex.
To not have sex.
God, this body feels free.
And what about wearing what I please—
colors painted down my leg, studs in my nose?

To exist here and now—
isn't that freedom?

To use my brain.
To think critically.
To be paid, heard, applauded, challenged—
and allowed to implement my education in everyday life.

My freedom, dressed in privilege—
does it come at the price of someone else's?
Who else gets to fuck up, ask forgiveness, and move forward?
How much of this world is still shadowed?
Too much.
Slavery still exists—and persists.

To own is to be free:
to own our thoughts, our bodies, our homes, our words,
our beliefs, our future, our finances.

Can freedom be transferred?
What is the cost of the transaction?
Because my free is not always your free.

I see, and hear, and feel
how the world still withholds its allowances on freedom.

There is something kindling in the ashes.
Fire roars when our voices rise, fanning the flames.
Still I wonder—
as I ride the upward heat of my subjective freedom—
when will it all burn down?

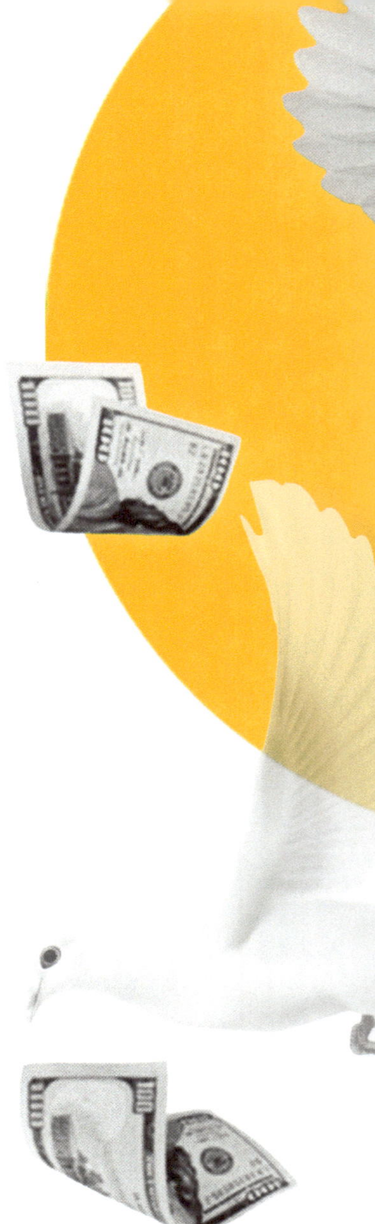
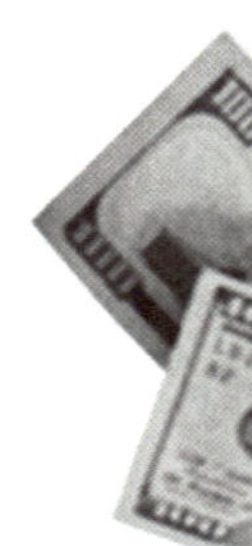
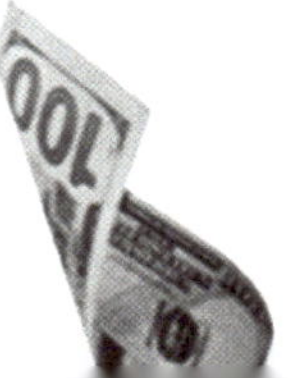

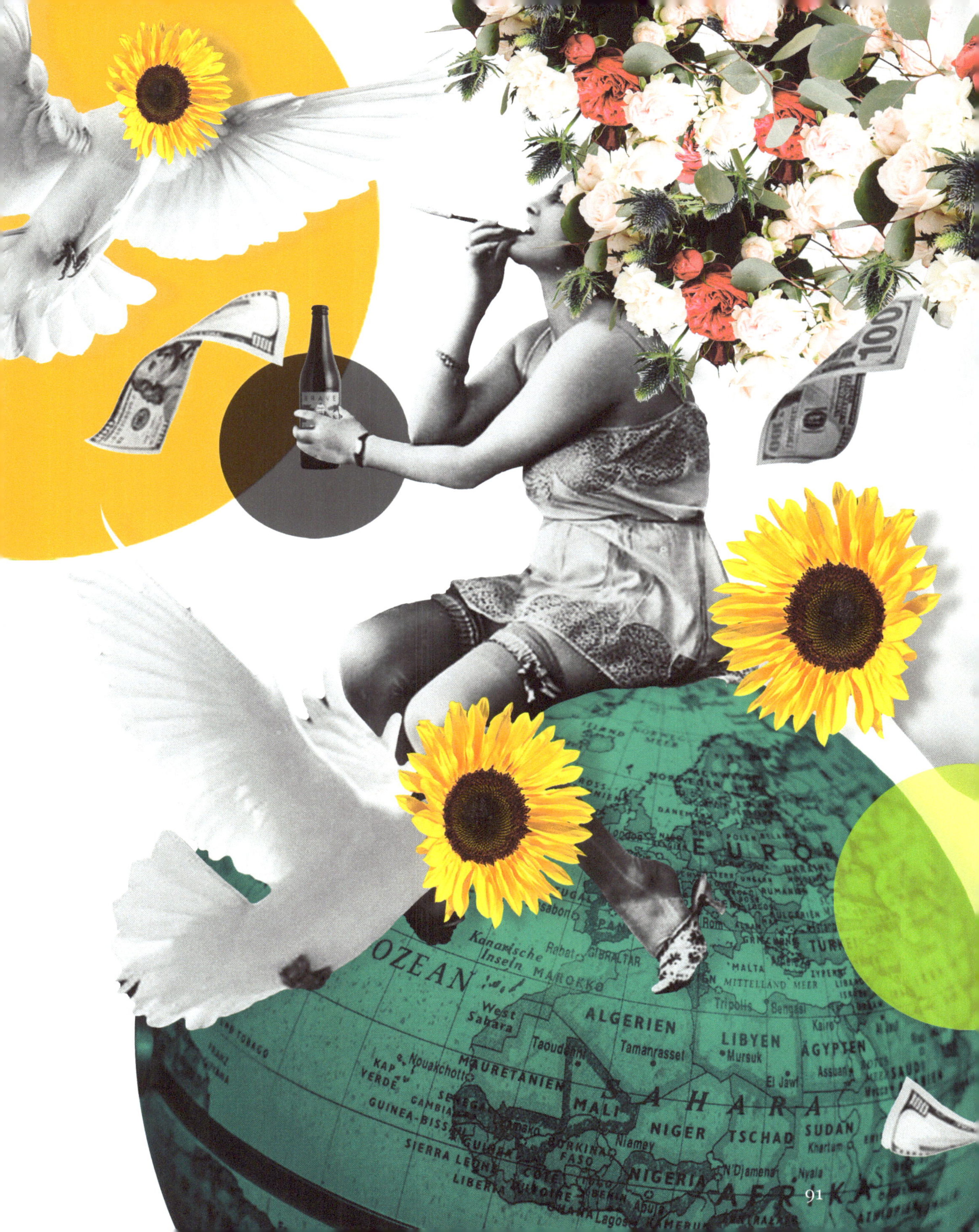

OZEAN
Kanarische Inseln
Rabat GIBRALTAR
West Sahara
MAROKKO
KAP VERDE
Nouakchott
MAURETANIEN
SENEGAL
GAMBIA
GUINEA-BISSAU
SIERRA LEONE
LIBERIA
Taoudenni
MALI
ALGERIEN
Tamanrasset
NIGER
BURKINA FASO
Niamey
NIGERIA
S A H A R A
LIBYEN
Tripolis
Mursuk
Bengasi
TSCHAD
N'Djamena
Nyala
SUDAN
Khartum
ÄGYPTEN
Kairo
Assuan
A F R I K A
EUROPA
POLEN
UKRAINE
RUMÄNIEN
Rom
TÜRKEI
MALTA
MITTELLAND MEER

Shmetterling

One of my favorite words translated across multiple languages is butterfly. In French, a butterfly is called papillon. In Spanish, it's mariposa. In Arabic, farasha. In Italian, farfalla. Regardless of a user's command of the language, the three or four syllables carry a similar tone of ease when articulated. Each syllable floats when spoken out loud, similar to the cadence of a butterfly flapping its wings. The word, when crossing the borders of another language, maintains a feeling of gentle beauty. Each designed with lyrical tones devoid of rigid consonants.

Author Steven Pinker's insight into writing style illustrates how the phonetic charm of a word like butterfly carries a poignant feeling by design. In his writing guide, *The Sense of Style,* Pinker states that the right word for a reader evokes a feeling of sound. "The best words not only pinpoint an idea better than any alternative but echo it in their sound and articulation... It's no coincidence that haunting means haunting and tart means tart and not the other way around; just listen to your voice and sense your muscles as you articulate them."[46]

As writers, we can magnify feelings for our readers when drawing on the lyrical landscape of a vast lexicon. Paying attention to the juncture of short and long vowel sounds, exploring the pit-pat of our t's and the buzz of our z's, we orchestrate imagery as well as feeling on the page. With intention, we can conduct a textual symphony to mesmerize our readers as opposed to bore them.

In today's exercise, let's play with language and sound by writing poetry.

Definition:

▸ Phonesthetics: the study of beauty and pleasantness associated with the sounds of certain words or parts of words.

Set Your Intention For Today's Writing Practice

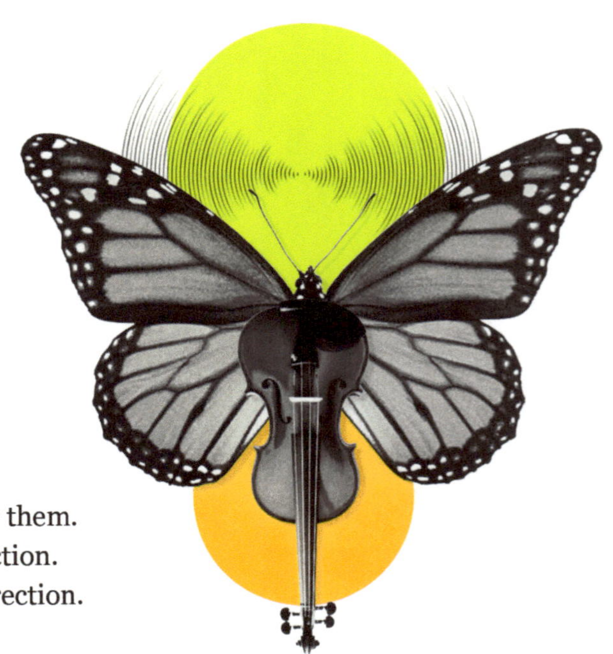

Your Writing Ritual:

▸ Stand with your arms out to the sides.
▸ Slowly trace large circles in the air with your fingertips as you breathe.
▸ Inhale as you lift your arms, exhale as you lower them.
▸ Continue for four full circles in a clockwise direction.
▸ Repeat four full circles in a counterclockwise direction.
▸ Let your arms fall gently to your sides.

Set your timer for 2 mins.
Answer the following question.
What does picking the "right word" look like in your writing process?

Set your timer for 2 mins.
Create a list of words associated with sound. Examples: woosh / buzz / echo / bellow

Pick an animal.

Set your timer for 2 mins.
Jot down how your animal from [Activity Two] moves through the world.

Set your timer for 2 mins.
Jot down how your animal from [Activity Two] sounds.

Endurance Writing Prompt:
Set your timer for 15 mins.
Write a poem about your animal from [Activity Two]. Help us as the reader understand how this animal moves through the world [Activity Three] and how they sound [Activity Four] by choosing verbs that mirror feeling. Challenge yourself to break up your poem using each of the 25 letters of the alphabet to start a new line or new stanza in your poem.

Guiding Questions:
What verbs can you draw from that describe sound and movement?
What would it look like if your animal behaved in the opposite manner you'd expect it to?

It's All Play

When writers are set loose for fifteen minutes of endurance writing in my workshops, the energy shifts. Writers hunch over their papers, biting their lips in thought, holding their foreheads perhaps in mystery, until eventually each is enthralled, their pens scribbling in haste. They want to be here—it's not a class. They're more receptive to working past the discomfort of awkward first thoughts on the page because they like how it feels to have written. What I love is how their body language, their focus, mirrors the playful, transitive state you might catch a toddler in while they're hosting a tea party for their dolls or running to the playground to build an imaginary world with their friends.

I know this feeling of losing yourself to imagination. On the playground, I was a master storyteller, my first taste of plot-driven imagination came from conducting narratives on the playground. Surrounded by trees and a sea of gravel, the top floor of the fort was a moldable set. I could be at one moment a dragon guarding the castle and the next a train conductor in another child's idea of our play's plot. To play was to be involved, no matter the direction—a system and a state of mind.

Writing is, in its own form, a way of playing—in production and state of mind. We take to the page as writers, engaging with ideas, in a kind of play where words take the direction of our imagination.

In today's exercise, let's explore the literal play from your childhood to play with the blank page.

Set Your Intention For Today's Writing Practice

Your Writing Ritual:

- ▶ Stand or place your feet flat on the floor.
- ▶ Roll your shoulders in a backward circular motion.
- ▶ Repeat for four deep breath cycles.
- ▶ Reverse the motion of your shoulders.
- ▶ Repeat for four deep breath cycles.
- ▶ Drop your shoulders and shake out your hands.

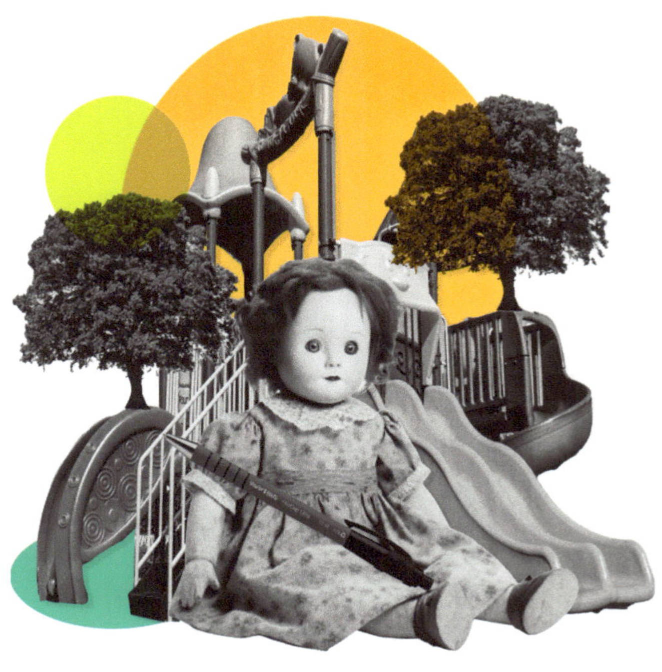

Your Warm-Up:
Set your timer for 2 mins.
Answer the following question.
What does it mean to play?

Activity One:
Set your timer for 2 mins.
Make a list of all the ways you liked to play as a kid. Examples: playing house / playing scientist / playing accountant / playing the boss of my younger siblings

Activity Two:
Pick one form of play from your list in [Activity One].

Activity Three:
Set your timer for 2 mins.
Based on your selection from [Activity Two], jot down specific activities involved in this type of play. Examples for playing accountant: itemizing plastic fruit / creating invoices for my stuffed animals / creating printer paper checks / signing my name on everything and everywhere

Activity Four:
Set your timer for 2 mins.
Make a list of reasons why your play might have been interrupted. Examples: nap time / older sibling crashed the party / someone said play was for babies / dinner time

Endurance Writing Prompt:
Set your timer for 15 mins.
Write a nonfiction account of being enthralled with play as [Activity Two]. Write your way into memories around this type of play by painting a picture of what this play looked like for you [Activity Three]. Allow us as the reader to be there with you and understand what might have disturbed your state of play [Activity Four].

Guiding Questions:
What are your hands doing as you play? Your feet?
How do you feel now as an adult, reflecting on this type of play from your childhood?

What's In A Name

I was looking for English titles in a bookshop deep in the old walled city of Cartagena, Colombia, when I pulled a book from the shelf upside down. I continued to run my fingers along the bindings of a thousand various voices under one brick roof, pulling more titles. One after another, each book on the shelf sat bottom up.

Taking a step back, I understood how this strange design made the titles of each book easier to read. In English, we read from left to right. Naturally, we would tilt our heads to the left, wanting to read a title on its side. I pondered all the ways we as writers think about how readers take in our titles—now dizzy with the idea of how even the slight tilt of the head affected a reader's impression of a book.

Your work eventually faces the world under a title. With one line, your art moves to inhabit the world in a great quest to be consumed. We, as the reader, decide to commit to an experience of reading by simply being partial to a book's title. Yet, for as much importance as titles carry, among peers, there is a lack of a concrete formula for creating a title.

I've worked with writers whose work sprouted from a title. Others find the title buried in the shallow depths of a final draft. A few who have plucked their titles from the ether for mere convenience, an afterthought, before sending their work to a publication. Some writers hear the whisper of the title in a dream, while others fixate on capturing an entire movement of feeling in four words. Then you have authors whose work exists in the world as untitled altogether. Titles can mean everything and nothing to a piece of work, but to a reader, they have the designation of carrying an entire story in one breath.

In today's exercise, let's work backward to explore fictional writing sparked by titles.

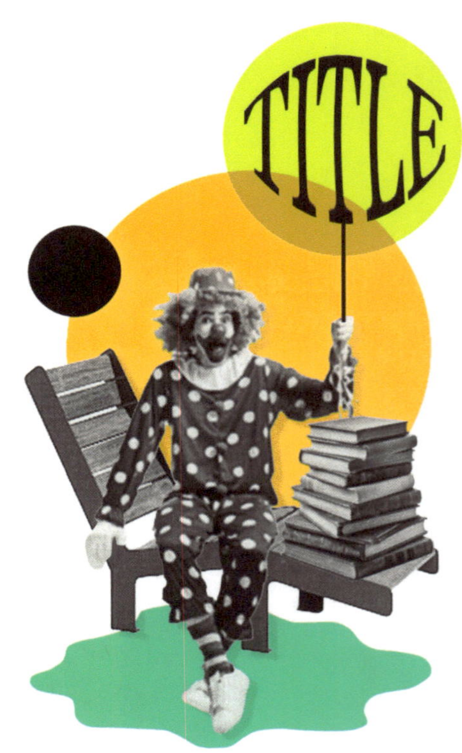

Set Your Intention For Today's Writing Practice

Your Writing Ritual:

► Sit or stand with your eyes closed.
► Visualize a still lake.
► Inhale and imagine the surface calming.
► Exhale and feel your body become still.
► Repeat this visualization and breath pattern for five cycles.
► Open your eyes slowly.

Set your timer for 2 mins.
Answer the following question.
What are your criteria when picking a new book to read?

Activity One:
Set your timer for 2 mins.
Make a list of as many movie and book titles as you can think of.

Activity Two:
Set your timer for 2 mins.
Make a list of obscure book topics. Examples: a love of cannibalism / the history of clowns / backyard suntans / human behavior based on phases of the moon

Activity Three:
Choose one obscure topic from [Activity Two].

Activity Four:
Set your timer for 2 mins.
Create as many original titles as you can in relation to this obscure topic. Examples for the history of clowns: The Frowny Clown / Water Once a Week / A Humble History From Clown Town / Happiness Hurts: A History of Clowns

Activity Five:
Choose a title from [Activity Four].

Activity Six:
Set your timer for 2 mins.
Jot down a list of questions a writer might set out to answer in a book about your obscure topic from [Activity Three]. Examples for the history of clowns: Who was the first clown? / How did the profession of clowning come to be? / Why do clowns scare people?

Endurance Writing Prompt:
Set your timer for 15 mins.
Imagine you're pitching a new book [Activity Five] to an editor. First, you must summarize the book's premise. Work to convince the editor of why readers need this book on [Activity Three] by diving into the questions your book will cover [Activity Six].

Guiding Questions:
What will readers miss out on knowing if you don't write this book?
How can you show the editor that your title will pull readers in?

Clickbait

There are 990 words in the English language that begin with the letter V. A number, I was stunned to discover. Rattling through a few words beginning with the letter V, I discovered how delicious V words sound when read aloud. The delicate contact between your bottom lip and upper front teeth, combined with the gentle exhale of the consonant V, is just downright playful. Consider reading this aloud. One of my favorite verbal parades of the letter V comes from the movie *V for Vendetta*.

"The only verdict is vengeance; a vendetta, held as a votive, not in vain, for the value and veracity of such shall one day vindicate the vigilant and the virtuous. Verily, this vichyssoise of verbiage veers most verbose, so let me simply add that it's my very good honor to meet you and you may call me V."[62]

The passage reminds me of the beautiful relationship between writing and reading aloud. I love imagining how some mechanics in writing are entirely playful, rhythmic for both reader and writer. Alliterations like the monologue above allow words to move. In writing, we can bring images to life outside of plain language and revive our imagination through wordplay.

In today's exercise, let us play with alliteration to create copy that moves our fingers and our mouths.

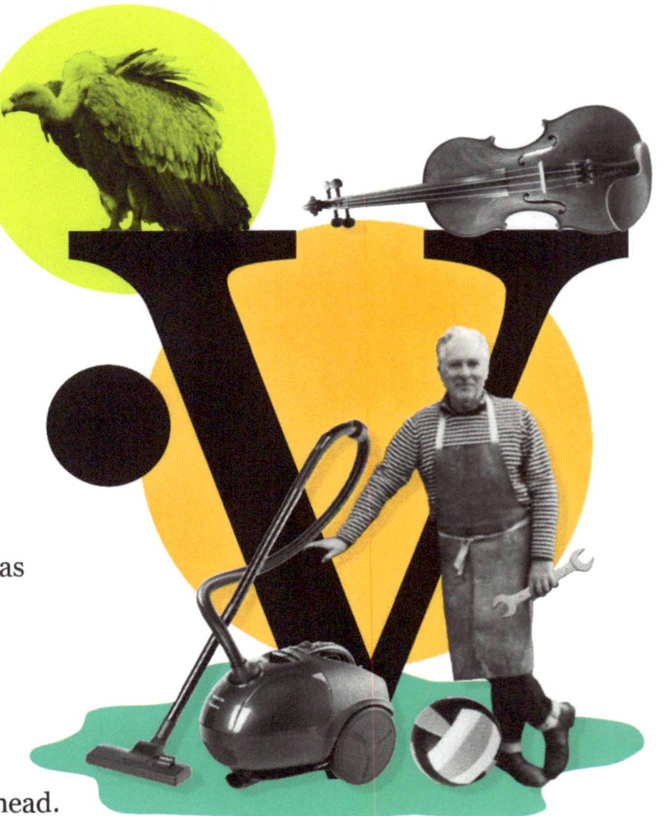

Set Your Intention For Today's Writing Practice

Your Writing Ritual:

- Sit in a chair with a tall spine.
- Close your eyes and imagine your thoughts as bubbles floating away.
- Inhale deeply through your nose.
- Exhale slowly and mentally "pop" one thought bubble.
- Continue this visualization for five breaths.
- Open your eyes and stretch your arms overhead.

Set your timer for 2 mins.
Answer the following question.
Where would be the best place on earth to read a favorite book passage or monologue aloud?

Activity One:

Set your timer for 2 mins.
Open a book to a random page. You can use this book if you don't have access to another at the moment.
Pick one word from the page that draws your attention.

Activity Two:

Set your timer for 2 mins.
Make a list of words that begin with the same letter as well as words that carry the same sound as the word from [Activity One].

Activity Three:

Set your timer for 2 mins.
Make a list of stories that might be considered worthy of a daily newspaper article. Example: bank robbery / Renaissance Fair / a teacher suddenly takes up the tambourine / bread becomes the world's strongest currency

Activity Four:

Choose a storyline from [Activity Three].

Activity Five:

Set your timer for 2 mins.
Create an alliterative headline for this story idea. Use words from [Activity One]. Example:
Bank Busted By Breakout Blondes / Rats Rummage Rochester Renaissance Rendezvous / Teacher Takes Tutelage To The Tambourine / Bread Breaks Banks For Best Business Buy

Endurance Writing Prompt:
Set your timer for 15 mins.
This just in [Activity Five]! You're a news reporter of some seriously juicy news. Create a report of the event. Set the scene. Give us the facts, and make the story dance with alliterative language [Activity Two].

Guiding Questions:
How can you weave in the who, what, when, where, why of the event to keep your alliteration moving along?
How might the story change based on what kind of readership you are speaking to?

The Dog Goes Guk Guk

I stood on the sidewalk gripping my backpack full of our electronics and our passports—anything I could grab in the state of emergency. A searing fire alarm in our apartment building in Da Nang had triggered tenants to take to the street. My husband, dog, and I joined our Vietnamese neighbors Lan and Nguyen, who were in their pajamas empty-handed. A bit shaky, I wanted to ask our neighbor about their cat, but I didn't speak Vietnamese, which made the question more ambiguous both to ask and answer. I opted for a light "meow" sound with a few hand licks to complete the charade before shrugging. Lan nodded and then responded with her own sound of "meo," more of a short vowel sound that tugged my ear. She pointed up to the fifth floor of our building where they lived. Lan, apparently, knew two things I did not: one, fire alarms were nothing to worry about, and two, cats did not "meow" in Vietnam.

The more I traveled, the more I discovered variations in the barnyard sounds I'd learned as a kid. In Korea, a cat goes "yaong yaong." The bark of a dog in Indonesia is "guk guk," and the oink of a pig in Albania is "hunk." A mouse in English would "squeak," but in German it goes "piep-piep." The discovery that basic onomatopoeia animal sounds might vary by country was exciting, like finding another octave in one's voice, more dimension to something exhausted and cataloged.

In writing, onomatopoeia is more than the "boom" or "pow" of a comic book. We can use sounds to give more dimension, to send chills up the reader's spine in a mystery novel or amplify the drama of a scene in a mental hospital. Your setting can have a voice—the screech of the subway tracks, the chime of a bell tower, the sputtering of an espresso machine.

In today's exercise, let's play with onomatopoeia to flip conventional sound association and have more fun writing.

Definition:
▸ Onomatopoeia: the formation of a word from a sound associated with what is named

Set Your Intention For Today's Writing Practice

Your Writing Ritual:
▸ Stand with your feet hip-width apart.
▸ Inhale while reaching your right arm up and over your head for a side stretch.
▸ Exhale and return to center.
▸ Inhale and stretch your left arm over.
▸ Exhale and return.
▸ Repeat this flow four times on each side.

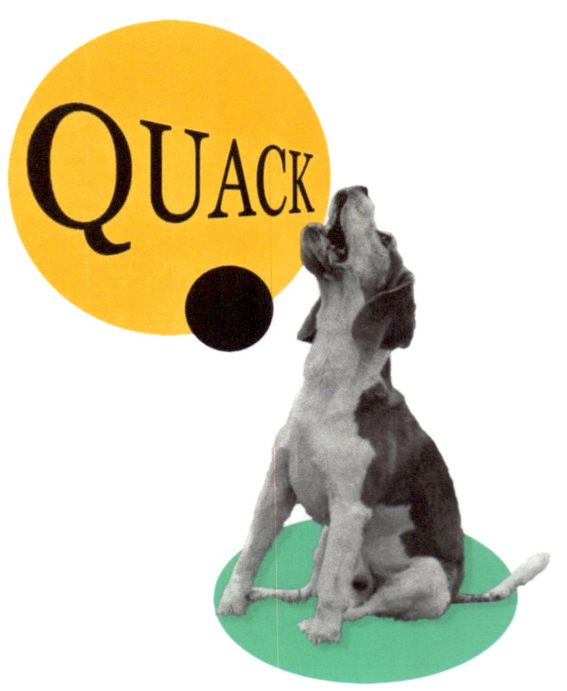

Your Warm-Up:
Set your timer for 2 mins.
Answer the following question.
What sounds can you hear?

Activity One:
Set your timer for 2 mins.
For each of the onomatopoeias below, list an action or a noun that you would normally associate with this sound. Example: squish—banana
Bing   Click   Whoosh   Boom
Thwack   Pew   Snap   Cluck

Activity Two:
Set your timer for 2 mins.
For each of the onomatopoeias below, list an action or a noun that you would not normally associate with this sound. Example: squish—stone
Bing   Click   Whoosh   Boom
Thwack   Pew   Snap   Cluck

Activity Three:
Set your timer for 2 mins.
Make a list of possible reasons why the world as you know it might be lucid or off-kilter.
Examples: on drugs / pulled into a movie / entered a new dimension / traveled to a foreign planet

Activity Four:
Choose a reason from [Activity Three].

Endurance Writing Prompt:
You are the main character of a setting where the sounds around you are off from what you know because of [Activity Four]. You are in a new place where everything from the cluck of a chicken to the swoosh of the wind are off-kilter. Drop into a scene where you are moving about this world, experiencing sound in a whole new way. Try to include as many of the inverted onomatopoeias [Activity Two] as you can.

Guiding Questions:
Who else is in this setting experiencing the oddity of new sounds?
How does your perception of the world change the more new sounds that you hear?

The Last Lick

The New York Times article headlined "National Park Service Asks Visitors To Please Stop Licking Toads."[40] After a moment to re-read the title, my tongue felt rigid with the metallic taste of an imagined toad's spine dragged across the surface. Then I had a dozen questions. The article names the growing wellness retreat industry as the culprit. Soul seekers flock to the Colorado desert, paying thousands of dollars for a ceremony of psychedelic experience. The toxin is scraped from the toad's back, dried, and then smoked. Rich blokes smoking dried toad toxin? Psychedelic toads at risk? Then I wondered, why aren't there more stories about tongues?

Salacious intentions aside, the tongue and our taste buds are one of the five core senses to experience the world. Yet, unless it's a riveting novel with a chef as a protagonist, tongue time is subservient to the nose when image casting as a writer. However, when we look at the animal kingdom, we know dozens of species use their tongues to function outside of the last lick of an ice cream cone. Apes, canines, felines, and even birds use their tongues to gather information and heal wounds. The muscle in their mouth is for sensory exploration. As outlandish as the toad lickers in the *Times* article may be, they spark a sense of wonder in how we might alternately experience the world.

In today's exercise, let's give the tongue its time by creating modern-day fables about licking what we shouldn't.

Definition:
▸ Fable: a short story, typically with animals as characters, conveying a moral.

Set Your Intention For Today's Writing Practice

Your Writing Ritual:
▸ Sit and place your feet flat on the floor.
▸ Lay your hands, palm-side up, on your knees.
▸ Breathe in through your nose to the count of four.
▸ Breathe out through your mouth to the count of five.
▸ For each breath in, focus on the palms of your hands.
▸ Repeat your breathing cycle until you feel a warmth starting in your hands.

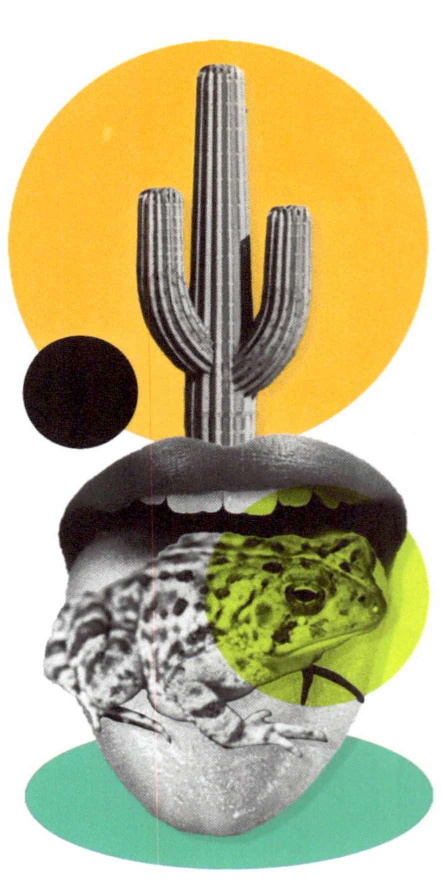

Your Warm-Up:

Set your timer for 2 mins.
Answer the following question.
What was your favorite short story as a kid?

Activity One:

Set your timer for 2 mins.
Describe your favorite taste in the world? Example: The tang of a freshly brewed Colombian light roast coffee coupled with rich heavy cream.

Activity Two:

Set your timer for 2 mins.
Make a list of things you shouldn't lick. Examples: rocks / frozen telephone poles / your boss's nose / a stranger's ice cream cone

Activity Three:

Pick one item you shouldn't lick from [Activity Two].

Activity Four:

Set your timer for 2 mins.
What is a consequence, real or imaginary, someone might experience if they licked the item picked in [Activity Three]. Example for rocks: getting sick / growing rock warts / rocks growing in your belly / rocks getting offended

Activity Five:

Set your timer for 2 mins.
What sensory exploration might someone be doing as they lick something? Example: dared / curious about the mossy texture / bubble gum residue / wondering what last night's rain tastes like

Endurance Writing Prompt:
Set your timer for 15 mins.
There's just too much licking going on in town. People are using their tongues for extended sensory exploration [Activity Five]. When one individual gains a fascination with licking [Activity Three], the town decides something must be done. The town believes that too much licking can lead to consequences of [Activity Four]. Drop us into a fable of what really happens in the town of the last lick.

Guiding Questions:
Who convinced your protagonist to do the licking?
What should we learn as the reader from your fable of The Last Lick?

Thumbstacks In Time

I work with a handful of writers who prefer memoir. The most common mistake I coach on is where the prose lags, where the narrative latches on to unnecessary notches in their timeline. The tricky aspect of memoir is figuring out how to pinpoint the events threading your personal story while resisting the urge to regurgitate every detail in your life.

A mentor of mine, author and poet Sue Guiney, inspired my favorite memoir exercise for writers when she shared a first draft of her poem at the time called "Bloomberg." She marked her life in tandem with who was in office as mayor for milestones in her history. I loved the parallel between the personal and the historical. I loved the way she patterned, dressed, and unpacked her vulnerability in growing up in the city while confidently tying herself to the timeline of New York. She refined decades of narrative into tightly bound stanzas.

Memoir is palatable to most writers. Good memoir happens when your personal story becomes personable, anchoring your narrative in either a theme or timeline your reader can step into and draw meaning from.

In today's exercise, let's use universal time markers as a way to tell a story about our lives with a wide lens.

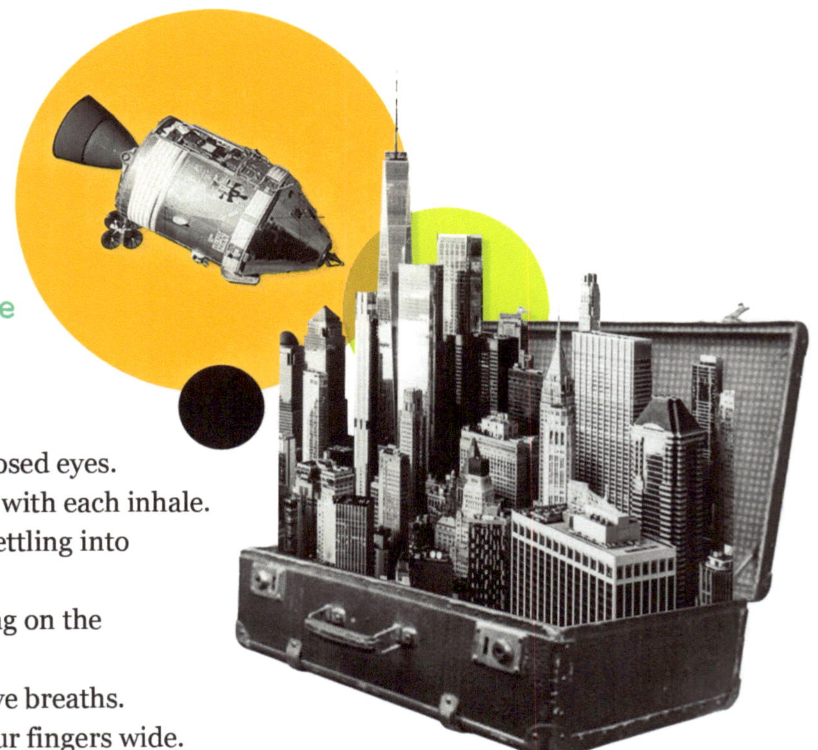

Set Your Intention For Today's Writing Practice

Your Writing Ritual:

- Sit with a straight spine and closed eyes.
- Imagine a warm light entering with each inhale.
- Exhale and imagine the light settling into your chest.
- Breathe in light, exhale focusing on the ground beneath you.
- Repeat this visualization for five breaths.
- Open your eyes and stretch your fingers wide.

Write faster than your editing brain dares to keep up with.

Set your timer for 2 mins.
Answer the following question.
What was popular in the decade you were born?

Activity One:
Set your timer for 2 mins.
Make a list of universal time markers throughout history. Examples: presidents / Apple products
/ internet advancements / natural disasters

Activity Two:
Pick one of the time markers from [Activity One].

Activity Three:
Set your timer for 3 mins.
Expand on the time marker you picked from [Activity Two], capturing significant changes you can
remember. Examples for Apple products: colorful iMac desktop monitor / iPod / iWatch /
Find My iPhone update

Activity Four:
Set your timer for 3 mins.
For each of the time markers above, tie in one significant memory from your life at that time.
Examples for Apple products: colorful desktop monitor—I wore teal fake reading glasses.
/ iPod—I first heard the term pocket rocket. / iWatch–I went to summer camp for kids with
Ulcerative Colitis / Find My iPhone update—I moved out of my parents' house.

Endurance Writing Prompt:
Set your timer for 15 mins.
Create a poem about your life through the lens of a universal time marker from [Activity Two]. For
each time marker you identified in [Activity Three], connect a moment about your life to that time
[Activity Four]. Allow flow to trump structure or style.

Guiding Questions:
How did your personal style change when time markers changed?
Why did things change?

Water Cooler Whispers

I labored on a short story called "Her Garden" for a year. I wrote dozens of revisions, recasting the life event of a city woman in her 40s returning to her hometown to settle her mother's estate. My protagonist is convinced she needs to tend to the magnificent garden, but her days in the soil are long gone. To spice up the drama, the protagonist's mother bequeathed her lover the house and the garden. I worked on the imagery of the garden, of loss, drawing up friction between characters, stirring pain, and stoking disaster. I tried different dramatic reveals, multiple endings, added characters, then deleted them, but the piece continually twisted in my gut. I read and re-read the piece out loud until the lines became familiar. The familiarity unearthed a realization—a feeling.

Author Anne Lamott writes about this feeling when you're reading aloud and "hit a patch of dialogue that is so purple and expositional... suddenly the piece is emotionally tone-deaf."[31]

I realized the piece faltered in the dialogue. My characters spoke exclusively for plot. I had crafted two broken characters ready to fight to the death over who was more admired, but their exchanged lines existed for exposition. I ignored the instinct to listen to my characters. Moreover, I neglected to listen to conversations in the buzzing world around me. Without a well of conversation to draw from, my default was to plot.

Believable dialogue is a necessary cornerstone in writing well. You must fine-tune your ears. Lean into the quarrel of worn lovers in the grocery store and the hyper hum of teenagers in the mall. You'll collect the compost of conversation needed to write believable dialogue when the time comes.

In today's exercise, let's play with conversation between colleagues whose loose lips bring high gossip.

Set Youir Intention For Today's Writing Practice

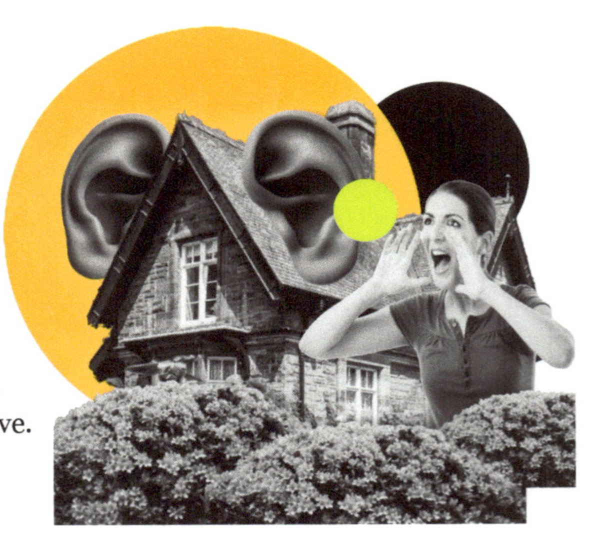

Your Writing Ritual:

- Stand or place your feet flat on the floor.
- Rise onto your toes and hold.
- Breathe in through your nose to the count of four.
- Breathe out through your mouth to the count of five.
- Bring your heels back to the floor.
- Repeat this cycle four times.

Set your timer for 2 mins.
Answer the following question.
What's your attitude toward small talk?

Activity One:
Set your timer for 2 mins.
Make a list of actions, thoughts, or observations when you know you've said the "wrong" thing out loud in public. Examples: scoff / the wide eyes of people around you / the elbow nudge in the ribs by a friend / a quick snap back by someone else

Activity Two:
Set your timer for 2 mins.
Make a list of scandals that employees might gossip about regarding their place of work. Examples: boss slept with a coworker / someone replaced the tea in the break room with weed / newest coworker is a stripper on the weekend / last employee fired had it coming

Activity Three:
Choose a scandal from [Activity Two].

Activity Four:
Set your timer for 1 min.
In reference to what you picked in [Activity Three], what is one thing you would absolutely not want to say out loud if someone asked you about the scandal?

Endurance Writing Prompt:
Set your timer for 15 mins.
It's the end of a long week as your character and their coworkers head out for a few drinks, which turns into one too many. Suddenly, the office's biggest scandal [Activity Three] bubbles to the surface. Your character says [Activity Four]. Jump into the scene. Put us right at the table where your character has just opened their mouth. Write the scene unafraid of creating conflict. Keep the story moving through open dialogue.

Guiding Questions:
Why has your character shared their opinion?
What does their dialogue lead us to believe about who they are?

A Passenger

I fell into the novel, *On The Road* by Jack Kerouac, during a year of reading on a massive scale. I set out to consume any and all books I could lay my hands on. The novel was a title I heard whispered in literary circles or referenced in movies. I'd spent over a decade living outside the US, largely on the move. I figured the novel was right up my alley. I liked the idea of status in being someone who had read Kerouac's iconic '60s novel known for capturing the Beat Generation. I savored the flipped frame of capturing the world from the passenger seat.

Our protagonist and narrator, Sal Paradise, is a passenger—hitchhiking, bussing, walking—in a journey from New York to San Francisco inspired by his carefree friend Dean Moriarty. All manner of plot unfolds. No matter the deficit to our character's ego, the loss, the heartbreak or absurdity, Sal returns to the road, to motion, but continually as the passenger. He's chasing freedom and spiritual understanding, but he can never quite take the wheel of the present moment. He's convinced that if he can just keep moving on to the next moment, then life is on the other side: "I was halfway across America, at the dividing line between the East of my youth and the West of my future."[25]

There is the past and there is the future, yet the entire novel is of the present, painted with somewhat disdain, as he moves from city to city, party to party, seeking self. Sal's view of the world as a passenger gives us a unique perspective of the road when you relinquish control in an effort to continue moving.

As a writer, you can use the proverbial passenger seat to explore how your characters react in situations of transition. You can strip characters of control and place them in high-stress scenes—a bus barreling down the narrow mountains of Peru or stuck in a traffic jam during the last jaunt of a cross-country drug run. You can, as they say, torture your characters to see how they respond. However, to craft a believable literary voyage, let's build first from a nonfiction lens.

In today's exercise, let's explore observations from the passenger seat.

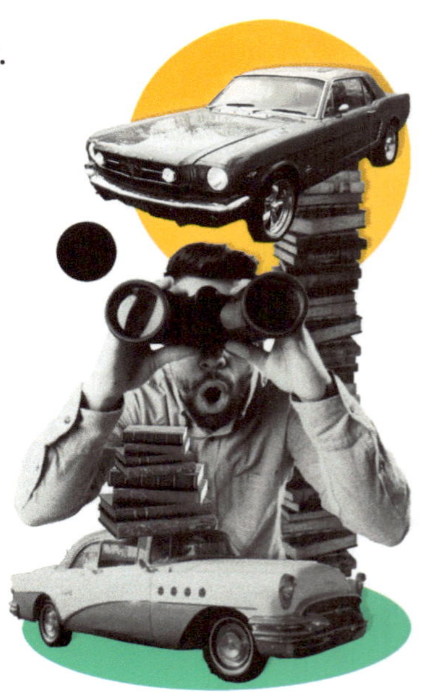

Set Your Intention For Today's Writing Practice

Your Writing Ritual:
- Sit or stand with your spine straight.
- Bring your fingertips to your temples.
- Inhale deeply, pressing gently.
- Exhale and slowly slide your fingers along your hairline to your jaw.
- Repeat this calming stroke for five breath cycles.
- Release your hands.

Your Warm-Up:

Set your timer for 2 mins.
Answer the following question.
When was the last time you were a passenger?

Activity One:

Set your timer for 2 mins.
Make a list of types of transportation where you've been a passenger of. Examples: virtual spaceship / camel
/ bed of a pickup truck / motorbike

Activity Two:

Choose one type of transportation from [Activity One].

Activity Three:

Set your timer for 2 mins.
Make a list of things you can do as a passenger while being transported by the vehicle you chose in [Activity
Two]. Examples: sleep / lead road trip games / point out every Texas license plate / navigate incorrectly

Activity Four:

Set your timer for 2 mins.
Make a list of things you do not have control over as a passenger while being transported by the vehicle you
chose in [Activity Two]. Examples: speed / smell / awkward conversation / seating arrangement

Endurance Writing Prompt:

Set your timer for 15 mins.
Being a passenger affords you the power of observation. Begin to isolate one specific memory of
traveling as a passenger by means of the transportation you chose in [Activity Two]. Ease into a
journal entry of a memory. Show us what is possible, within your control [Activity Three], and
what elements of the journey are out of your control [Activity Four]. Build from a place of where
you were headed and who is driving.

Guiding Questions:

How were you keeping your hands busy as the passenger?
Why does this memory pull forward when you think about the transprtation you picked?

Juicy Subject Lines

Part of my position at The American University in Vietnam was to run writing workshops for university freshmen. On a day I called in sick, my boss, Dr. John Behzad, eagerly jumped at the opportunity to lead a writing workshop. He has a doctorate in economics, but the written word is his obsession. His fascination with a singular sentence in a book on writing fueled his excitement for an entire hour over tea one afternoon. Behzad's workshop, the day I was out sick, was a micro view of writing in the world of business. His theme was on emails. A bore of a subject, and yet the Alka-Seltzer of his enthusiasm was evident. I know because back in the office, we reviewed his workshop, tossing ideas back and forth on how to standardize the excitement of email writing for the whole of the university. Dr. John Behzad believed there was magic behind a well-written email, and he was determined to break the magic down to replicable science.

I would be lying if I said I thought emails were magical. I imagine you're groaning at even the mention of the word, but what if an email, the format of an exchange between two servers at the hands of a need to communicate, was the place to begin telling a story? Writing in all its forms can be exciting. Emails can create magical outcomes: connecting with a long-lost relative, getting Human Resources to respond to a complaint, sharing recipes for goulash, or confirming a trip to Tokyo. Email format offers an interesting platform to begin weaving a new tale.

In today's exercise, let's explore a more exciting side of writing emails.

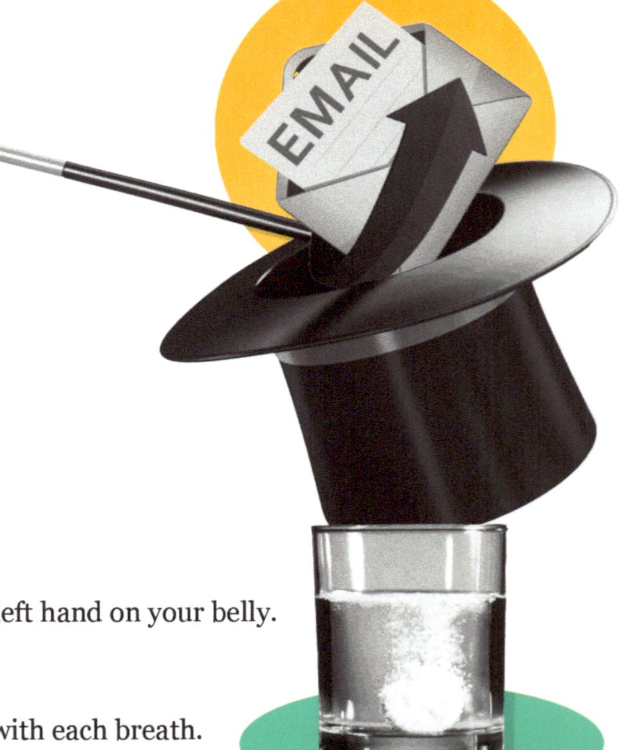

Set Your Intention For Today's Writing Practice

Your Writing Ritual:
- Sit tall with your feet flat on the ground.
- Place your right hand on your chest and your left hand on your belly.
- Inhale slowly, noticing which hand rises first.
- Exhale fully and feel both hands fall.
- Focus on syncing both hands to rise together with each breath.
- Repeat for six breath cycles.

Your Warm-Up:
Set your timer for 2 mins.
Answer the following question.
Why do you use email?

Activity One:
Set your timer for 2 mins.
Make a list of all the reasons why you send and receive emails. Examples: request information / ordering a cheesecake / filing a complaint / confronting your wife's lover

Activity Two:
Set your timer for 2 mins.
Make a list of things that would be uncomfortable to discover over email. Examples: a breakup / death announcement / confession of someone's alien encounter / your accountant telling you to file for bankruptcy

Activity Three:
Choose one topic from your list created in [Activity Two].

Activity Four:
Set your timer for 2 mins.
Bulletpoint the outline of an email around the topic picked in [Activity Three]. Consider the interrogative questions if you're stuck (who, what, when, where, why, and how).

Activity Five:
Set your timer for 1 min.
Explore different ways to turn the topic from [Activity Three] into the subject line of an email.
Examples: It's Not You, It's Me / Mama Bit The Dust This Morning / Does Putting Out Count As Love? / It's True... They're Out There

Endurance Writing Prompt:
Set your timer for 15 mins.
It's Thursday at the office. You're settling into the groove of work. You're not enjoying the thought of checking your inbox, but an email catches your eye. The subject reads [Activity Five]. It can't possibly be a legitimate email, but your fingers can't resist. You click open the email and begin to read about [Activity Three]. Use your outline [Activity Four] to construct the email within your story.

Guiding Questions:
What is the monologue in your head while you're reading this email at work?
What is the concluding sentence of the email, the call to action?

Heat On Your Heels

Summers in the suburbs meant bike rides and crawdad fishing in the creek. My heart raced with joy when my feet were naked. I liked a little heat on my heels. I preferred to parade my toes in the grass. My father had a rule that to leave the house, we had to have shoes on. A working-class man, I saw his toes only on vacation. I snuck out the back door and somehow always managed to leave my shoes at home. Barefoot, I ran faster. Barefoot, I made up songs in the garden. Barefoot, I believed I was wild.

As an adult, I walk barefoot on the beach near my house. I have forgotten the rush from feeling life between my toes. My Qigong teacher, Dee, sends me to the water to be still, to notice the sounds, the vibrations, and the warmth of energy moving around me. He knows that I write well after I've found my footing. He's led me to a practice in grounding for better writing. Similar to Buddhism, drawing energy from the earth is ancient practice. Grounding is a central component to finding balance before moving forward.

Often, as writers, when we've stolen twenty minutes to write, we fail to quiet our minds from the frazzled state of our regular day. However, when we can be intentional about the transition between the busy and the creative mind, we are more productive. When we can pause to feel the earth below us, we can remember we are supported. We are held up by the ground at our feet. We are stable, steady, to let writing come through us like a channel. We are ready to be wild in our writing.

In today's exercise, let's write about the ground beneath us.

Set Your Intention For Today's Writing Practice

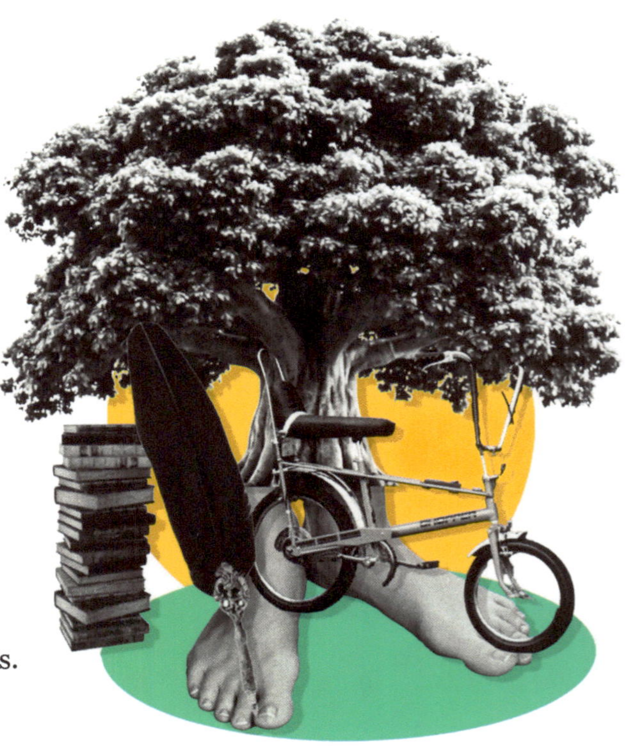

Your Writing Ritual:

- Stand with your feet hip-distance apart.
- Allow your arms to move freely side to side.
- While moving your arms to the left, inhale.
- While moving your arms to the right, exhale.
- Repeat the breathing and movements six times.
- Shake out your hands.

Set your timer for 2 mins.
Answer the following question.
When was the last time you went barefoot outside?

Activity One:
Set your timer for 3 mins.
Make a list of all the thoughts running through your head on a busy day. Examples: to-do lists / song fragments / numbers / criticism

Activity Two:
Set your timer for 3 mins.
Take off your shoes and socks. Make a list of what you feel and your reactions as your feet are naked to the ground. Examples: cold tiles / grains of sand / tendency to stretch / big toes tapping

Endurance Writing Prompt:
Set your timer for 15 mins.
Write a first-person nonfiction narrative where you move from a frazzled state of mind to a calm, grounded state of mind. Drop us into your thoughts [Activity One]. Then free your feet. Feel the ground underneath your toes [Activity Two]. Slow down your writing as your thoughts slow down. Allow us to see, hear, feel what you do.

Guiding Questions:
How are your emotions tied to your experience in grounding?
What happens when you close your eyes while you ground?

No BS When You Write

Did you know that Dr. Seuss famously wrote *Green Eggs and Ham* when the co-founder of Random House said it was impossible to write a story in book form with 50 distinct words or fewer? Or that Hemingway's six-word short story is legend to have come from a dare, and Mary Shelley's *Frankenstein* came out of a dare to write her scariest ghost story?

I am fascinated with the creative challenge each of these writers tackled to create the classic works we read today. Both Dr. Seuss and Hemingway completed their challenges under the guidelines of a maximum word count, a ceiling, but neither faltered in building the walls, the floors, the floorboards, or even the door of their strict writing challenge despite the limitation. Part of the charm of being a creative writer is to accept challenges as an invitation to play.

Challenging the boundaries of writing is part of creating, or in the case of my good friend Chris, a professor and writer, challenging the boundaries of writing was a way to flex his writing muscles after laboring through his first novel. He wrote on a self-prompted challenge of rewriting the story of *Snow White*, absent words containing the letter E. He wanted to work on something different and thought rewriting by restriction would be a fun way to play. Keep in mind, there are 347 words with the letter e in the classic version of "Little Snow White" by Jacob and Wilhelm Grimm. Not to mention the obvious part that he needed to rename his protagonist: *Snow White* transformed into Ivory Snow.

I love that Chris wrote on this challenge simply because he wanted to. Seuss, Hemingway, and Shelley all completed their dares, and in this fact, I choose to believe they enjoyed the play of writing. As writers, we have an inexhaustible source of play if we choose.

In today's exercise, let's challenge ourselves to rewrite classic fairy tales, restricting our word choice.

Set Your Intention For Today's Writing Practice

Your Writing Ritual:

- Stand tall and look toward the ceiling.
- Inhale deeply as you slowly tilt your head down to your chest.
- Exhale and turn your head to look over your left shoulder.
- Inhale and return to center.
- Exhale and turn your head to the right.
- Repeat this slow neck arc and side turn three times.

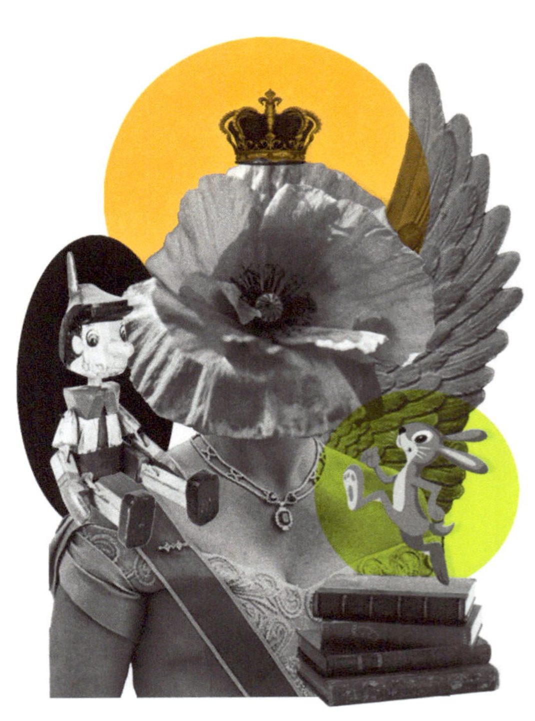

Your Warm-Up:
Set your timer for 2 mins.
Answer the following question.
What was your favorite children's story growing up?

Activity One:
Set your timer for 2 mins.
Make a list of classic fairytales or stories. Examples: *The Tortoise and The Hare* / *Cinderella* / Pinocchio / *Jack and the Beanstalk*

Activity Two:
Choose one classic fairytale or story from [Activity One].

Activity Three:
Set your timer for 3 mins.
Jot down the plot points of the classic fairytale or story from [Activity Two]. Examples for *Cinderella*: girl is bullied by step sisters / girl makes a wish / godmother grants girl a pumpkin carriage / girl fits in the glass slipper for a happy ending

Activity Four:
Set your timer for 1 min.
Review your plot points from [Activity Three]. Underline any words that begin with the letters B or S.

Endurance Writing Prompt:
Set your timer for 15 mins.
You are pioneering a new version of the classic fairytale [Activity Two]. Tell the tale using your plot points [Activity Three] as your outline. Rework a condensed version of the classic fairytale in your rewrite, avoid words with first letters B or S.

Guiding Questions:
What senses can you use to discover another B or S word?
How can you use a different attribute of the character to replace a B or S word?

Circles

The power of good writing is being able to dismantle complex ideology into consumable ideas. Time is one of those ideologies. As a construct, time has fascinated artists across the ages. Whether it's seeking ways to make up time like Kate Atkinson's *Life After Life*, manipulate time like H.G. Wells's' *The Time Machine,* or contemplate infinite time like in the Greek mythology of Sisyphus, writing serves as a medium to unpack the tumultuous relationship humans have with time.

As I read one of the thousands of juicy sentences in Viet Thanh Nguyen's book, *The Sympathizer*, his direct approach to time as the "open secret of the clock, naked for all to see, was that we were only going in circles,"[41] struck me. The complexity of time is made simple by its captive form— a circle, a clock, something we can see, hold.

The sticky relationship humans have with time is synonymous with the vulnerability of being naked, a feeling we can step into as the reader. The cyclical nature of the clock becomes a race where, for those who are looking, finding irony—distance brings one back to the beginning. A line continuing forever. A clock, no longer a clock, but a relentless secret keeper, amused by our perpetual hurry to lap another circle. With one sentence, as the reader, we can inhabit the range of feelings around time while grounded in the physical reality of a clock. Nguyen's prose dresses the abstract concept of time in the concrete, familiar shapes around us.

In today's exercise, let's explore writing poems relying on the shapes around us to write about time.

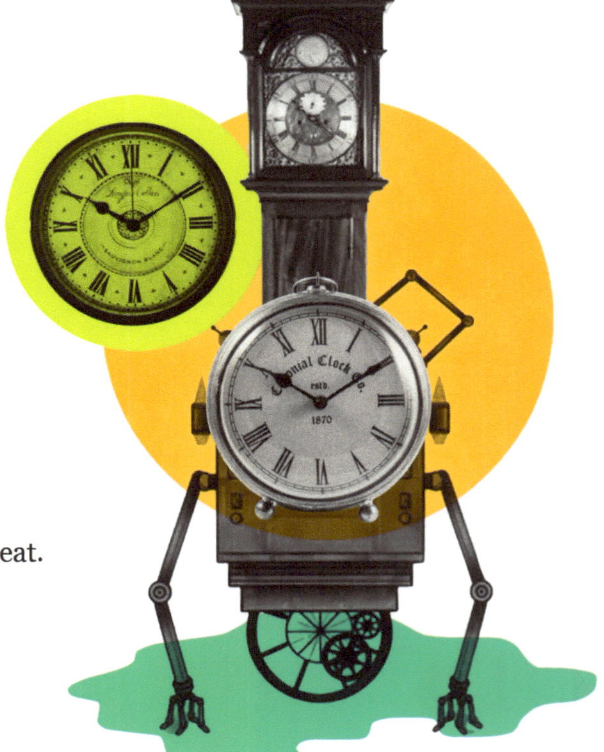

Set Your Intention For Today's Writing Practice

Your Writing Ritual:

- Stand or sit upright.
- Rub your hands together quickly until you feel heat.
- Place your warm palms lightly over your eyes.
- Inhale through your nose and exhale slowly through your mouth.
- Hold this position for three breaths.
- Drop your hands and shake them out.

Set your timer for 2 mins.
Answer the following question.
What do you do with your free time?

Activity One:
Set your timer for 2 mins.
Make a list of common phrases about time. Examples: running out of time / time knows all / time wears on / in the interest of time

Activity Two:
Set your timer for 2 mins.
Write down instances where someone is counting time. Examples: New Year's Eve countdown / cooking / running on a treadmill / a loved one is sick

Activity Three:
Set your timer for 2 mins.
Make a list of 2D and 3D objects that have a round shape. Examples: smiley face emoji / peach / moon / hole in my jeans

Activity Four:
Set your timer for 2 mins
For each of the round shapes in [Activity Two], add a description of feeling and sight. Examples: smiley face emoji—joy, yellow / peach—hungry, fuzzy / moon—somber, blinding / hole in my jeans—lazy, tattered

Endurance Writing Prompt:
Bring these two odd ends of thinking—roundness and time—into the body of a poem. Start each stanza with a phrase from [Activity One] and use an example of counting time from [Activity Two] to support your phrase. Expand your creativity to paint an image around time using concrete shapes and descriptions from [Activity Four].

Guiding Questions:
If you could hold time in your hands, what would you do?
When do you feel the most at ease with time, and what does that look like in the form of an object?

Notes

Numbers refer to quotations used in the text; all other works listed here were referenced but not directly quoted.

1. Atkinson, Kate. *Life After Life*. Reagan Arthur Books, 2013.
2. Atwood, Margaret. *Negotiating with the Dead: A Writer on Writing*. Anchor Canada, 2002, p. 35.
3. Benjamin, Chloe. *The Immortalists*. G.P. Putnam's Sons, 2018.
4. Bradbury, Ray. *Zen in the Art of Writing: Essays on Creativity*. Bantam, 1992, p. 13.
5. Bradbury, Ray. *Zen in the Art of Writing: Essays on Creativity*. Bantam, 1992, p. 36.
6. Chen, Eva. *Juno Valentine and the Magical Shoes*. Illustrated by Derek Desierto, Feiwel and Friends, 2018.
7. Dahl, Roald. *Charlie and the Chocolate Factory*. Puffin Books, 2001, p. 86.
8. Doerr, Anthony. *Cloud Cuckoo Land*. Scribner, 2021.
9. Donoghue, Emma. *Room*. Little, Brown and Company, 2010.
10. "For sale: baby shoes, never worn." Attributed to Ernest Hemingway.
    See Smith, Graeme. "Baby Shoes, Never Worn: Hemingway's Six-Word Story and Internet Folklore."
    Journa of Minimalist Literature, vol. 4, no. 1, 2012, pp. 14–22.
11. Gaiman, Neil. "October Tale." *A Calendar of Tales*, Neil Gaiman, 2013,
    https://acalendaroftales.com/october.
12. Gallico, Paul. *Confessions of a Story Writer*. Doubleday, 1946, introduction.
13. Gilbert, Elizabeth. *Big Magic: Creative Living Beyond Fear*. Riverhead Books, 2015, p. 108.
14. Gilbert, Elizabeth. *Eat, Pray, Love: One Woman's Search for Everything Across Italy, India and Indonesia*. Viking, 2006.
15. Gilman, Charlotte Perkins. "The Yellow Wallpaper." *The New England Magazine*, Jan. 1892, pp. 647–657.
16. Goldberg, Natalie. *Writing Down the Bones: Freeing the Writer Within*. Shambhala, 2005, p. 147.
17. Golding, William. *Lord of the Flies*. Faber and Faber, 1954.
18. Grimm, Jacob, and Wilhelm Grimm. "Little Snow-White." *Grimms' Fairy Tales*, translated by Margaret Hunt, George Bell and Sons, 1884, pp. 198–209.2017.
19. Guiney, Sue. "Bloomberg." Unpublished manuscript.
20. Hanks, Tom. "Tom Hanks: Uncommon Type." *Beautiful Writers Podcast*, hosted by Linda Sivertsen, episode 21, 17 Oct. 2017. Apple Podcasts,
    https://podcasts.apple.com/us/podcast/tom-hanks-uncommon-type/id1047012231?i=1000394239140.
21. Hemingway, Ernest. *A Moveable Feast*. Edited by Sean Hemingway, Scribner, 2003, p. 12.
22. Heston, Charlton. "America's First Freedom." Speech at the Harvard Law School Forum, 16 Feb. 1999. Transcript available via NRA.org archives.
23. Higginson, Chris. "Ivory Snow." Unpublished manuscript.
24. "I hate writing. I love having written." Attributed to Dorothy Parker.
25. Kerouac, Jack. *On the Road*. Penguin Books, 1991, p. 138.
26. Kesey, Ken. *One Flew Over the Cuckoo's Nest*. Viking Press, 1962.
27. King, Martin Luther, Jr. "I Have a Dream." *The Civil Rights Movement: A Photographic History, 1954–1968*, edited by Steven Kasher, Abbeville Press, 1996, pp. 88–92.
28. King, Stephen. *On Writing: A Memoir of the Craft*. Scribner, 2000, p. 145.
29. King, Stephen. *On Writing: A Memoir of the Craft*. Scribner, 2000, p. 157.
30. King, Stephen. *The Shining*. Doubleday, 1977.
31. Lamott, Anne. *Bird by Bird: Some Instructions on Writing and Life*. Anchor Books, 1995, p. 64.
32. Lamott, Anne. *Bird by Bird: Some Instructions on Writing and Life*. Anchor Books, 1995, p. 178.
33. Lewis, C. Day. *The Poetic Image*. Jonathan Cape, 1947.

34. Mailer, Norman. Interview by Jean Malaquais. *Writers at Work: The Paris Review Interviews, Second Series*, edited by George Plimpton, Viking Press, 1963, p. 219.

35. Mansbach, Adam. *Go the F** to Sleep**. Illustrated by Ricardo Cortés, Akashic Books, 2011.

36. Monsen, Avery, and Jory John. *All My Friends Are Dead*. Chronicle Books, 2010.

37. Monsen, Avery, and Jory John. *K Is for Knifeball: A Book of Terrible Advice*. Chronicle Books, 2012.

38. Morrison, Toni. Interview by Pam Houston. "Toni Morrison Talks Love." *O, The Oprah Magazine*, Nov. 2003, pp. 270–276.

39. Moyes, Jojo. *Someone Else's Shoes*. Pamela Dorman Books, 2023.

40. "National Park Service Asks Visitors To Please Stop Licking Toads." NPR, 3 Nov. 2022.

41. Nguyen, Viet Thanh. *The Sympathizer*. Grove Press, 2015, p. 199.

42. Nguyen, Viet Thanh. *The Sympathizer*. Grove Press, 2015, p. 321.

43. Nguyen, Viet Thanh. *The Sympathizer*. Grove Press, 2015, p. 359.

44. Ogawa, Yōko. *The Memory Police*. Translated by Stephen Snyder, Pantheon Books, 2019.

45. Orwell, George. *1984*. Harvill Secker, 1949.

46. Pinker, Steven. *The Sense of Style: The Thinking Person's Guide to Writing in the 21st Century*. Penguin Books, 2015, p. 22.

47. Poe, Edgar Allan. "The Murders in the Rue Morgue." *The Complete Tales and Poems of Edgar Allan Poe*, Vintage Books,   1975, pp. 123–154.

48. Pullman, Philip. *His Dark Materials*. Everyman's Library, 2011.

49. Robbins, Tom. *Skinny Legs and All*. Bantam Books, 1990.

50. Roberts, David Gregory, *Shantaram*

51. Sachar, Louis. *Holes*. Farrar, Straus and Giroux, 1998.

52. Scieszka, Jon. *The True Story of the 3 Little Pigs*. Illustrated by Lane Smith, Viking, 1989.

53. Seuss, Dr. *Green Eggs and Ham*. Random House, 1960.

54. Shelley, Mary. *Frankenstein; or, The Modern Prometheus*. Lackington, Hughes, Harding, Mavor & Jones, 1818.

55. Silverstein, Shel. *Falling Up*. HarperCollins, 1996.

56. Solnit, Rebecca. *The Faraway Nearby*. Viking, 2013.

57. Steinbeck, John. *Travels with Charley in Search of America*. Penguin Books, 1980, p. 104.

58. Swanson, R., and Jess Jansen. *Nobody Likes a Cockblock: The Reductress Guide to Dating, Sex, and Romance*. Dey Street Books, 2019.

59. Sword, Helen. *The Writer's Diet: A Guide to Fit Prose*. University of Chicago Press, 2016, p. 1.

60. Sword, Helen. *The Writer's Diet: A Guide to Fit Prose*. University of Chicago Press, 2016, p. 5.

61. Tolkien, J.R.R. *The Fellowship of the Ring*. Houghton Mifflin, 1954.

62. *V for Vendetta*. Directed by James McTeigue, written by Lana and Lilly Wachowski, performances by Hugo Weaving and Natalie Portman, Warner Bros., 2005.

63. Vuong, Ocean. *On Earth We're Briefly Gorgeous*. Penguin Press, 2019.

64. Wells, H.G. *The Time Machine*. Heinemann, 1895.

65. Wilde, Oscar. *The Critic as Artist*. In Intentions, James R. Osgood, McIlvaine and Co., 1891.

66. Wilde, Oscar. *The Picture of Dorian Gray*. Ward, Lock and Co., 1891.

67. Zusak, Markus. *The Book Thief*. Alfred A. Knopf, 2005.

Acknowledgements

What you hold in your hands took five years to find its voice. *Creative Kindling* would not have arrived here without a village of writers along the way. Though five years is far longer than planned, I have tremendous gratitude for the lessons I've learned along the way.

A huge thanks to my editor, my writing wingwoman, my creative partner at Ideas Write Now, the one and only Stephanie Shepperd. From the moment you sat down at my writing table with your cowboy boots in Vietnam, I knew you were a force. Your energy lights up any room, and your writing rolls off the page. This book would have had dozens of misplaced commas and a few missing "e" on the backend of the word breath without your sharp editing lens. Thank you for sitting side-by-side with me late into the evenings to edit seven drafts of this book.

To my illustrator and designer, Shann Whitaker, you are an absolute legend. Is there nothing you can't do? Whether it's writing, illustrating, curating a banging Spotify playlist, or high-commercial art, you bring flair to everything you create. The collage style you came up with for this book elevated this project. You captured what it feels like to write in an Ideas Write Now workshop.
Thank you for all the extended effort to make this more than just a book of one medium. The full-page spreads of my poetry and your art are more than I could have imagined.

It's a long list of writers I'm grateful to have met, learned from, and written beside. Thank you to Andrew and Jessica for sitting at my table when I did not yet know how to facilitate. Thank you to Chris and Chris for giving the workshop its first home in Da Nang, Vietnam. I'll be forever grateful for Wednesday nights that brought us Evan, Anh, Kevin, Ryan, George, Rosaleen, Ben, Jenny, Sarah, Leah, Tyler, Hugh, and so many others. Thank you to Ky and Chris for our time in critique circles.

Thank you to Bondi Coffee for giving the Ideas Write Now workshop a table in Casablanca, Morocco. Tuesday nights of writing brought us Imane, Devon, Daniel, Elizabeth, Meredith, Katrina, Marwa, Diane, Emma, and more. A special thanks to Laura Santi, whose vulnerability in her writing always awes me and whose dedication to the group inspired Ideas Write Now's first free library. Thanks to Laura, Elisabeth, and Imane for carrying on the Ideas Write Now legacy in Morocco.

Lastly, to my incredible husband, I love you. Thomas, you show up to workshops, week after week, year after year, writing even when you say you're not a writer. Thank you for the unwavering support in my dreams. You've never doubted my voice. You've always been the first listener and my guiding feedback.

Now this book is out in the world, and a younger version of me is over the moon. My sincerest gratitude to you, dear writer, for choosing to embark on more creativity in your busy everyday life.

Thank you.
Happy writing!

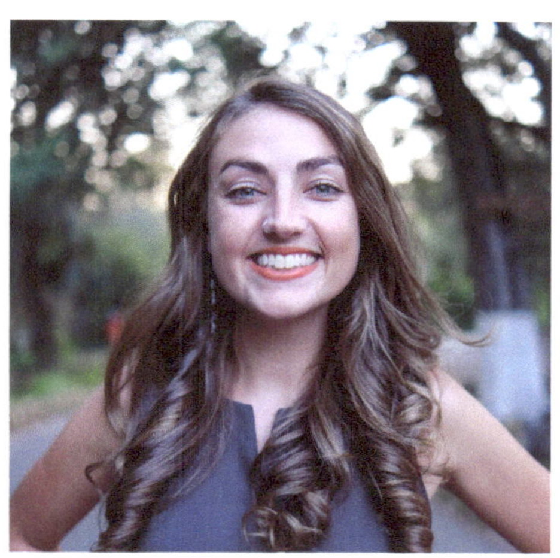

Rose Hedberg is a published co-author of flash fiction, an experienced freelance writer, ghost writer, and grant writer. Since 2017, she's been hosting creative writing workshops to help busy writers carve out time to get into the flow state. Rose has helped hundreds of individuals navigate their writing roadblocks to find more creative joy with her company, Ideas Write Now. Currently based in Colombia, Rose is a book fanatic collecting passport stamps every chance she gets. She lives with her husband, Thomas, and their two rescue dogs, Tocineta and Chicharrón.

@ideaswritenow
info@ideaswritenow.com
www.ideaswritenow.com

www.ingramcontent.com/pod-product-compliance
Lightning Source LLC
Chambersburg PA
CBHW041640110726
48005CB00003B/666